Stop Screaming!

A Beginner's Guide to Homemade Ice Cream

Benjamin M. Weilert

Non-fiction by Benjamin M. Weilert:

Stop Screaming! A Beginner's Guide to Homemade Ice Cream
This is Not a Drill
Cinema Connections: a never-ending "6 Degrees of Kevin Bacon"
Fourteener Father: a memoir of life above 14,000 ft.

Fiction by Benjamin M. Weilert:

Buried Colony
The Ascent of the Writer

The Fluxion Trilogy

First Name Basis
Second to None
The Third Degree
also available…
The Fluxion Trilogy Omnibus (with Appendix)

Connect with the author online!
www.benjamin-m-weilert.com

ISBN: 8397584227
ISBN-13: 979-8397584227

DEDICATION

To my lovely wife, Laura,
who started us on this delicious journey.

CONTENTS

Stop Screaming!

Chapter 4: Combinations 50

Contents

Chapter 5: Serving/Menus

Acknowledgements
About the Author
Non-fiction by the Author
Fiction by the Author

PREFACE

I have a distinct memory of homemade ice cream when I was growing up. It required a motorized bucket, a bag of rock salt, and some milk. Somehow, it always ended up tasting like peppermint, which was weird because I never recall any peppermint candies being added to the mix. I don't think there was any specific thing that triggered us making it, but I enjoyed that refreshing taste of homemade ice cream when it happened.

Fast forward a few decades, and my palate had grown slightly more sophisticated. I had made it a point to try all the different flavors of Ben & Jerry's ice cream that were available at the grocery store to determine which was my favorite. In no particular order, my top three were S'mores, Cinnamon Roll, and Red Velvet Cake. I'm sure if I had eaten the same summer ice cream from my childhood, I would have found it bland and uninteresting in comparison.

Then, I got married.

I'm a mechanical engineer who has little patience for exact science. However, my wife has the precision that came from an education deep in chemistry and biology. This came in handy because she is excellent at baking (an exact science) and I'm good at making dinner (often an in-exact science). Of course, my penchant for sweets meant I never complained when she would bake something out of the blue for us to eat.

In creating the registry for our wedding, we realized we already had most of the things we'd need to establish a household together. In fact, we had multiple copies of these items. We figured we should ask for gifts that would build upon what we already had.

"You have that Kitchen-Aid Stand Mixer, right?" my fiancée at the time asked.

"Yeah. A bachelor can have a stand mixer. What of it?"

"I'm not saying it's not masculine, but what if we asked for the attachments?"

Having seen the variety of attachments for this device, I thought this was a good idea and put them on our wedding registry. We got a lot of use out of at least a few of the attachments we received as gifts, but the one we use the most is the ice cream maker.

The first batch of ice cream my wife made was an instant hit. It was a simple, no-cook vanilla that used 20-year-old aged vanilla extract from Mexico. I took the first bite of this batch and thought to myself, *There's no way I'm going back to store-bought ice cream.* Over the next few months, she experimented with recipes, trying to recreate some of my favorite Ben & Jerry's flavors with varying levels of success.

When Independence Day rolled around, we were ready to have a housewarming for the new home we had bought. Because we hadn't completely unpacked or prepared to entertain guests, we made it a simple party with friends and family. Aside from the standard cookout/grilling food, we served a variety of flavors of homemade ice cream we had made. The ice cream social portion of our party was a hit, so we made it an annual tradition. Fourth of Jul-ice Cream was born.

There were only five flavors for our first event in 2015. Cherry chocolate chip, strawberry, cinnamon, double chocolate, and vanilla. In 2023, we have expanded to 17 different flavors, and that was even leaving some off the list that had made appearances in previous years.

We learned a lot about homemade ice cream during that first event. The most important lesson was that we didn't need guests to bring toppings like you would if you were eating the cheapest grocery store vanilla ice cream. In fact, the flavors my wife had created were so rich and complex that the toppings did a disservice to them.

These ice creams can stand on their own.

After years of refining our craft and puzzling through some challenges, my wife and I have made at least six dozen different ice cream recipes in total. There have been plenty of mistakes throughout this process, as well as fantastic recipes that are lost to time after we forgot to write them down.

This is why I wrote this book.

I didn't want any more recipes or techniques lost, so I picked my wife's brain, and we came up with the basics for creating these ice creams. Through rigorous scientific testing, I refined these recipes to capture everything we have successfully made up to this point.

Through this book, I hope to educate those who want to make ice cream from home. For simplicity's sake, I'll be referring to both sorbets, sherbets, and ice creams as the cover-all term "ice cream." Where needed, I've added notations for sorbets and sherbets. I want to show how simple this process is, but also how to achieve some truly complex flavors through some ingenious methods. You'll hopefully benefit from our experience as you learn how to progress along your journey of homemade ice cream.

Don't take these recipes as the end-all-be-all here. See what works and explore new ways to add different flavors to your repertoire. We have been constantly adding to our bag of tricks for making ice cream and it's amazing to see how far we've come in eight short years. There are still techniques we want to test, like using soft drinks for flavoring the bases, making a spicy ice cream, or figuring out how to get the syrup swirl mix-in to be more consistent. The possibilities are nearly limitless and are all achievable with the foundations laid out in this book.

So, grab your milk, heavy cream, and sugar and stop screaming! You've got this!

Bon appétit!

Benjamin M. Weiler

How to Use this Book:

Each recipe in this cookbook provides ingredients and step-by-step instructions to follow. Variations to these recipes are noted after the instructions with the needed additional (or replaced) ingredients and modified steps. Further modifications for particular base/ mix-in combinations are noted in Chapter 4. The recipes in each section are ordered roughly in order of complexity (i.e., difficult recipes are later in the chapter).

Because modern food blogs have hidden the actual recipes beneath walls of anecdotal text, I put the recipes of this book front and center. If you're interested in the stories behind these recipes, be sure to read the **HERE'S THE SCOOP** notes. These provide background on how the recipes came about or what mistakes to avoid. For the mistakes I felt needed special recognition, please read the boxed **SHOUT OUT!** sections for sanity-saving tips.

CHAPTER 1: EQUIPMENT

I know it's tempting to jump right in and get to the part where you're tasting your very first batch of homemade ice cream. First, you must understand the equipment you'll need to make this happen. This section should enlighten you to the few things you may already have in your kitchen, as well as the things you might be missing. As a note, if I call a brand name out for a piece of equipment, it's merely the one that we use. You might already have something better.

Of course, the most important item to make ice cream at home is none other than…

The Ice Cream Maker

This is a vessel that is used to churn the ice cream you've made. It uses a paddle to stir the un-chilled mixture past a chilled surface. As the mixture gradually cools, it eventually solidifies along the sides of the vessel as the temperature of the mixture drops below freezing. Let it run for long enough and the mixture turns into ice cream that is ready to eat. It is still likely to be too soft, which is why you'll want to pour the contents into a container and let it set in your freezer for a few hours.

The reason the ice cream maker vessel works is that it is colder than the mixture being poured into it. During my childhood, the bucket we used to churn our ice cream used a combination of ice water and rock salt to achieve this cooling effect. Modern ice cream makers are either self-contained refrigerated units or use refrigerant chemicals. These ensure the vessel is cold enough to achieve the desired effect.

Because this is the backbone of your ice cream making journey, modern ice cream makers can be expensive. Don't think you can save money here, as the cheaper you go, the better the chance that it will break. Even if the top-end ice cream makers sell for hundreds of dollars, our ice cream maker of choice is the Kitchen-Aid Stand Mixer attachment. This attachment currently costs about $80, but it is worth every penny. Of course, this is considering you've already made the $400+ investment in a Kitchen-Aid Stand Mixer. If you want just the ice cream maker without the mixer, there are options for standalone devices. A Cuisinart ice cream maker is around $70.

If you decide to read the reviews for this attachment, understand that this piece of equipment is sensitive to sudden changes in temperature. It's easy to break this device if you don't treat it with care and respect. Much like a high-quality Pyrex dish will still crack and break when put through direct, rapid heating, this device can crack and leak its coolant if you don't allow it to reach the right temperature gradually. As with any ice cream maker you choose to get, be sure to read through the manual and follow its instructions. They'll tell you how long to freeze it ahead of time, washing instructions, the capacity of the freezing vessel, and the allowed size of the mix-ins.

By now, you're probably wondering why anyone would ever heat an ice cream maker. The cleaning process of this vessel can be a bit time consuming, but there is a point where you apply warm, soapy water to ensure the vessel is ready to use again. If you were to pour this cleaning water into the vessel right after you've made your batch of ice cream[1], the ice cream maker will freeze it. This defeats the purpose of using warm water to clean the vessel.

The proper way to clean this vessel requires you to let it sit at room temperature until it has lost its chill. It is then safe to apply warm, soapy water to the vessel. Rinse it clean of the soap and wipe out any remaining moisture from the inside of the container. If any leftover soap residue remains, your next batch might not be as appealing. If there is moisture left in the vessel, it can freeze at the bottom and prevent the mixing paddle from sitting correctly for the next batch.

Do not succumb to the temptation to put this device in your dishwasher, as the heat of the dishwashing process will destroy it. As mentioned before, this is a piece of equipment that is sensitive to heat, so you will need to hand-wash it every time you use it.

After cleaning your ice cream maker vessel, it's a good idea to let it sit in your freezer for about 14 hours to charge the coolant. Be sure to read the instructions of your chosen ice cream maker thoroughly to determine the best way to care for it. It will let you know the recommended times it takes to fully churn a batch of ice cream.

SCRAPING SPATULA

My family has a little inside joke that was born when my mother was making something in the kitchen and asked us to hand her a spatula. Of course, spatulas come in more than one style. When we kept handing her scraping spatulas, she finally clarified, "Get me a flippin' spatula!" Us

---

[1] Which is a waste of the little extra bits of ice cream that you can scrape off and eat when you're done.

Stop Screaming!

young boys giggled at the euphemism, and it's stuck ever since.

You will not need a flippin' spatula for ice cream making, but you will need a scraping spatula. This is often referred to as a scraper. This spatula must have a solid handle and a firm silicone or rubber blade with a curved tip. If you can scrape out all the remaining ice cream from a vessel with this spatula, it is the correct one for our purposes here.

I'm 37 and—like most people over 30—have a favorite spatula. Unfortunately, I've already broken this spatula by accidentally trying to scrape a mix-in into the vessel as it was churning. Fortunately, they are fairly inexpensive. An OXO Good Grips® medium silicone spatula is my scraper of choice. It's 12-inches long, has a good grip (fittingly enough), and a firm but flexible blade.

An important reason to wash your spatula and ice cream maker vessel thoroughly after each use is the temptation to scrape out the remaining ice cream and lick the spatula clean. A quarter-serving of ice cream usually remains in the vessel after using it, so this is the time to taste it and make sure that everything is to your liking. If you're grossed out by this, maybe don't lick the bowl clean, but you're probably missing out on the joy that comes with making homemade ice cream.

Containers

Something you might not think about when you're preparing to make ice cream is where to put it when you're done. Sure, you can sit there and eat freshly churned ice cream right out of the ice cream maker. Unless you can down a whole quart of ice cream in a single sitting, you'll want to have a container to put in your freezer.

Most ice creams made with an ice cream maker will fit in a quart-sized container. Occasionally, the amount of volume that a mix-in adds to a recipe might require a larger container. No recipe in this book is ever more than about 1.5 quarts, so you should be fine if you have a variety of containers that can hold those two volumes.

Plastic containers are usually the best choice for this, but there are paper-based products out there that can hold a quart of ice cream. In our house, we use old containers of yogurt (1 quart) and cottage cheese (1.5 quarts). These wash well but do eventually wear out from being in the freezer all the time. The plastic will eventually crack, so you'll want to make sure you have enough of a supply to replace the ones that break. Similarly, paper-based containers don't always hold up under extended moisture and can tear when you scoop from them.

Measuring Cups & Spoons

Ice cream is a bit of an exact science, so having the right measuring cups and measuring spoons is important. Most recipes in this book will need a ¼-cup measuring cup for the sugar, a 2-cup measuring cup for the heavy cream, and (at a minimum) a teaspoon measuring spoon for flavor additives. For the 2-cup measuring cup, I prefer the Pyrex brand, especially if you can find the slanted design that allows you to see the measuring lines as you pour from above.

WHISK

Mixing liquid ingredients together is a requirement for making ice cream. A solid whisk ensures the mixture is even before letting it chill. Whisking also introduces air into the mixture, which creates an airy ice cream. While the size of the whisk is up to you, we use an 11-inch metal whisk to achieve the best results.

LARGE BOWL

Recall what I said about your ice cream maker being sensitive to hot temperatures? Before you pour your ice cream mixture into the chilling vessel, it needs to cool in the refrigerator. Any container that can hold the amount of liquid mixture is fine. However, sometimes it's best to just use the large bowl that you mixed the ingredients in and place it in your refrigerator. Most of these recipes will fit in a bowl that can hold 2 quarts, but if you want more margin for error, use bowls larger than that. Be aware that metal bowls will chill faster for non-cooked ice cream bases but might need to chill longer for cooked bases. A Pyrex, glass, or ceramic bowl is preferred.

Additionally, be sure your bowl has a lid or cover since the mixtures are going to be in the refrigerator for several hours. Even if your bowl does not come with a lid, you can use saran wrap or any variety of elastic covers to protect the contents of your bowl.

With these five pieces of equipment, you should be able to make your first basic ice cream. The rest of the equipment you'll need will help you with slightly more complex bases and mix-ins. Many of these items you may already have, but some have special uses that are specific to the process.

Meat Tenderizer

You are more than welcome to include meat (like bacon) in your recipes[2]. For this book, a meat tenderizer is useful for breaking up large chunks of materials used for mix-ins. Alternatively, you can use the bottom of a frying pan, or some other heavy object in your kitchen.

Thermometer

Ironically enough, an analog candy thermometer is the simplest way to tell if the ice cream base you're making is at the right temperature[3]. This is key for recipes requiring the addition of eggs, as it prevents you from making an omelet ice cream[4].

Digital thermometers can also work, but sometimes are more expensive and don't read the higher temperatures needed for some recipes (the Syrup Swirl mix-in [*pg. 47*], for example).

---

[2] After cooking it properly first.
[3] Or if the meat you're putting in your ice cream is fully cooked. Again, not recommended, but you do you—I'm not wild about bacon anyway.
[4] You can do whatever you want, don't let this book stop you.

Scale

A few recipes in this book require you to measure out ingredients by weight. While you can certainly guess on some of these measurements, it's better to be exact. A simple digital scale that can change units between ounces and grams is preferred.

Saucepan

Much like everyone over 30 has a favorite spatula, I would wager that most people also have a favorite saucepan. If you don't, you'll want to make sure you get one so you can make many of the ice cream bases in this book. I prefer the non-stick variety (either anodized or Teflon), but this is not a requirement. A 3.5-quart saucepan should be sufficient, but having a variety of sizes will make some recipes easier.

Double Boiler

A double boiler is likely the second most specialized piece of equipment on this list—right behind the ice cream maker itself. This item uses steam created in the bottom pan to heat the materials in the top pan evenly. I use the double boiler for the chocolate-based recipes as it prevents the chocolate from getting too hot in any one location on the pan and scorching.

There aren't too many different options for this piece of equipment, but if you find yourself without one you can alternatively use a metal bowl set on top of a saucepan of boiling water.

Potato Masher

Again, I'm not sure why you'd do this—other than to have a series of Thanksgiving ice creams—but you can make a mashed potato ice cream. I'd advise against it, and this cookbook does not have a recipe for it. Many of the fruit-based sorbets in this book require the use of a potato masher. It ensures the maximum juices and pulps from these fruits are available for the sorbet mixture. We find the waffle head mashers are best for this purpose.

Strainer

Impurities in ice cream can be a real turnoff. The sorbet recipes and the ones that require eggs are usually best if you use a strainer to filter the contents. This will remove any large pulp, seeds, or accidentally cooked eggs from the mixture before putting in the refrigerator to cool. An 8-inch wire mesh strainer (or similar size) is sufficient.

Blender/Food Processor

A good blender or food processor helps to return candies to a sugar-like consistency. This device also pulverizes the cream cheese or pulp sorbet recipes into smooth mixtures. We were fortunate to have been gifted the Ninja BL770 Mega Kitchen System as another wedding gift. We use this device for all our blending and food processing needs. While this setup costs a few hundred dollars, anything that can blend and will hold the required volume for blending (around 4 cups) should be sufficient.

BAKING SHEET & PARCHMENT PAPER

Some mix-ins for these recipes require time in the oven to remove their moisture (we'll talk about why in the mix-in section). You'll need a small baking sheet for these steps. More importantly, you'll want to put down parchment paper, so the sticky bits of fruit or chocolate don't stick to your pan. Otherwise, it's a pain to clean. You might also use a silicon sheet (Silpat is a common brand for these) instead of parchment paper. A half-sheet pan is more than sufficient. Sheets of parchment paper can be found at your grocery store and should be good for around 35 uses.

And that's it! Of course, you'll want a refrigerator (to cool mixtures) and freezer (to set the finished product and store the leftovers—whatever those are). I figure most homes have these amenities.

If you have none of this equipment and want to make ice cream from scratch, it should only cost you around $450 to buy everything mentioned in this chapter, assuming you already have a Kitchen-Aid Stand Mixer (at which point, it's closer to $900). Considering that you likely already have some of this equipment, it's probably going to cost considerably less. If you have a well-stocked kitchen already, you can get started for as little as $70 for the Cuisinart ice cream maker or $80 for the Kitchen-Aid ice cream maker attachment.

Now that we've covered what you'll need in your kitchen to make homemade ice cream, let's dive right in, shall we?

CHAPTER 2: BASES

I ce cream can be a bit like a building. You may have lots of fancy doors, windows, and walls, but if the foundation isn't solid, it won't really stand up against anything. The foundation of a good ice cream is its "base." This is the term I'll be using for the mixture that you will pour into your ice cream maker for the churning process.

You should be able to eat a base with no mix-ins and have it taste delicious. There are many variations for some of these bases, which are noted under the key ingredient for the recipe. Mix-ins will usually tweak the flavor profile and texture to create some wild creations. We'll get into these recipes in Chapter 4 [*pg. 50*], but for right now, we need to focus on the most important part of the home-made ice cream process. We'll start out simple and add some complexity throughout the chapter. By the end, you should be able to make a solid base that can rival anything you can buy at the store.

A house's foundation is made of concrete, which consists of three ingredients: water, aggregate, and cement. Similarly, the foundation of most ice creams consists of three ingredients: sugar, milk, and heavy cream.

For our ingredients, we use Zulka Morena Pure Cane Sugar instead of bags of granulated sugar. This is because it has a deeper flavor profile, the granules are larger so they dissolve in the base better, and it is closest to the pure form of the ingredient. We also prefer whole milk, as it contains more fat than 2%, Skim, or other non-dairy milks (which helps increase the needed fat content of the ice cream). We also like to use heavy whipping cream that is locally sourced, as it doesn't need as much pasteurization.

After you make a base, perform these seven steps to create your ice cream:

1. Cover the bowl holding the base and place it in the refrigerator for at least 4 hours to cool. You can also place the container you'll be using to set the ice cream in the refrigerator (along with the spatula used for scraping the vessel). This ensures the ice cream is being transferred to a cold container.

2. Once done chilling, whip the mixture with a whisk for about 30 seconds.

3. Pour chilled mixture into ice cream maker vessel.

4. Churn with ice cream maker until mixture solidifies. For the Kitchen-Aid attachment, the lowest "Stir" setting is the most consistent. You can increase the speed, which spreads the mixture further up the sides of the vessel but doesn't make the chilling process go any faster. Faster churns add more air into the mixture, resulting in more volume, so be sure to have enough space in your freezing container for the extra result. Be aware, though: faster churns with mix-ins may break the drive adapter. Other ice cream makers may not have different churning speeds, so be sure to check the manufacturer's instructions for how long it will take.

5. When mixture reaches a thickened consistency similar to soft serve ice cream that clings to the center of the paddle, stop churning. Check the instructions of your ice cream maker to learn the recommended churning time for your device.

6. Holding the vessel in your non-dominant hand, pour or scrape with a spatula from the vessel into 1-quart container. Have a small extra container

nearby if there is more ice cream than the container can handle.

7. Place the container in the freezer and let set for at least 8 hours before serving.

These seven steps are the same across each of these recipes and will appear as the step that says, "Chill, churn, and set." If you don't churn it for long enough, the result is still edible, even if its texture is less fluffy.

When the base is complete, scrape out the container and let it return to room temperature before handwashing. Chill in freezer for 14 hours prior to using again. Check with the manufacturer's instructions to ensure you're letting the vessel charge for the right length of time.

EXTRACT

INGREDIENTS:
- ¾ cup cane sugar
- 1 cup milk
- 2 cups heavy whipping cream
- Pinch of salt
- 1 Tablespoon flavor extract (choose one below):
  - Vanilla
  - Mint
  - Almond or Amaretto
  - Anise (i.e., licorice flavoring)
  - Root Beer
  - Cola

Stop Screaming!

Steps:

1. In a large bowl, whisk sugar and salt into milk until dissolved.
2. Add extract to heavy cream and stir.
3. Add heavy cream mixture to milk mixture and stir.
4. Chill, churn, and set.

Here's the Scoop:

Sometimes the mixture doesn't dissolve in the milk right away. Let it sit for a few minutes and whisk again until there's no more sediment.

Vanilla was the first ice cream my wife ever made for us. After one bite, I never wanted to go back to store-bought ice cream again. Some may consider vanilla to be plain, but when done correctly, it is amazing. It is an exotic spice, after all.

The key for us has been in the vanilla extract. We use 20-year aged Mexican vanilla extract for our recipes. This was because the bottle of extract we used was forgotten in a garage for 20 years. The temperature cycles of summers and winters in the arid Colorado climate helped to age this ingredient to perfection. Be careful, though, as it is much stronger than the vanilla extract you can buy at the grocery store, so don't go overboard with it.

Of course, after using up all our original stash of 20-year aged Mexican vanilla extract, we had to go back to get more. Even without being aged for 20 years in a garage, this extract is superior to the one you'll find at the grocery store. If you can get some, we highly recommend vanilla extract from Mexico.

In my family, we have an inside joke about vanilla extract because my mother typed out a recipe that called for it and was off by one key on her right hand. Instead of writing vanilla, she wrote vabukka. We still refer to vanilla as vabukka to this day.

You likely won't be able to find root beer or cola extract at the grocery store, but most home-brewing stores will carry these extracts. These stores may have other flavors as well, including grape and sarsaparilla. We only tested with root beer and cola, but let your imagination guide you to other flavors. This being said, do not use flavor infusers like Mio for this recipe. The result is likely to have an artificial and chalky aftertaste to it. Also, resist the urge to use a lemon extract, as there is a better lemon base further in this chapter (*see: Citrus Custard* [*pg. 28*]).

For the mint recipe, while grocery store mint extract can work fine for this recipe, it can sometimes leave a chemical aftertaste. As an alternative, you can also make a potent mint extract yourself at home. Since this extract isn't as strong, you must use 3 Tablespoons instead of one. Another alternative is to use 2 drops of peppermint oil instead of the Tablespoon of extract or 3 Tablespoons of homemade extract.

MINT EXTRACT

BONUS RECIPE

INGREDIENTS:
- 1 cup peppermint leaves (trimmed)
- 1 cup vodka

STEPS:
1. Trim peppermint leaves, making sure to cut the middle stem out.
2. Fill a jar with peppermint leaves and enough vodka to cover the leaves.
3. Let the jar steep in the refrigerator for 3 weeks.
4. Strain the leaves out of the jar and keep the remaining extract in the refrigerator.

CANDY

INGREDIENTS:
- ½ cup cane sugar
- 1 cup milk
- 2 cups heavy whipping cream
- 20 crushed candies, unwrapped [~100 grams] (choose one below):
    - Werther's Originals Caramels
    - Saltwater Taffy
    - Lemon
    - Peppermint
    - Butterscotch
    - Cinnamon
    - Blue Raspberry
    - Runts Fruit Candy

STEPS:
1. Using a food processor, pulverize candy into a powdered sugar. Combine with sugar.
2. In a large bowl, whisk sugar/candy mixture into milk until dissolved.
3. Add heavy cream mixture to milk mixture and stir.
4. Chill, churn, and set.

HERE'S THE SCOOP:
While all-natural ingredients are great, we could not recreate many flavors of ice cream without the aid of artificial flavoring. Since these artificial flavors are nearly impossible to find in the grocery store in their raw form, you must extract them from something else. Candies not only provide sugar to the recipe, but the artificial flavoring as well.

If you have the Ninja food processor setup, use the single serving cup to blend these candies.

Be sure to incorporate the candy sugar into the regular sugar before adding milk. Adding the candy sugar after the milk can sometimes cause it to clump up and fail to incorporate into the milk depending on the candy being used. Additionally, candies that are more waxy than hard—like jellybeans, licorice, and Lemonheads—are not recommended for this recipe.

The best candies for this recipe are hard candies. However, you *can* use softer candies like saltwater taffy for this recipe. With these softer candies, you'll want to unwrap and freeze them before pulverizing them in the food processor. By freezing them, the softer candies become brittle and easier to blend into a powder.

If you have a store that specializes in selling candy, you might find single saltwater taffy flavors there. However, since most stores don't sell single saltwater taffy flavors, we've consistently found buying in bulk from Amazon is the best way to get the flavors we want to use. While we've tried many saltwater taffy flavors, we've found the flavor of saltwater taffy that works best is cotton candy. Still, feel free to experiment with other flavors.

Ironically enough, when we tried to use actual cotton candy to add its artificial flavor to ice cream, the result was closer to bubblegum than the cotton candy flavor we were used to. You can try this method by following this recipe and replacing the candies with a bag of cotton candy.

Stop Screaming!

We have included many options for this recipe, but peruse the candy aisle at your grocery store to see what you can find and start experimenting! Be careful, though: while you can combine two or more different candies in a recipe (e.g., including all the Runts Fruit Candy in a batch), if there are too many flavors at once the result will be a "tootie fruity" base.

Cream Cheese

Ingredients:
- ¾ cup cane sugar
- 1 cup milk
- 1 cup heavy whipping cream
- 8 ounce package cream cheese (softened)
- Pinch of salt

Steps:
1. Blend sugar, milk, cream cheese, and salt in a food processor or blender until sugar is dissolved and mixture is smooth.
2. Add heavy cream and stir.
3. Chill, churn, and set. Due to cream cheese, requires less time to churn.

Here's the Scoop:
Using a food processor here makes this perhaps the easiest of all the bases to make. You can chill the base in the food processor container or transfer it to a clean bowl.

A cream cheese base is the foundation of cheesecake ice cream recipes. Mix-ins for these recipes will usually include crushed graham crackers [pg. 38] and your choice of fruit (e.g., strawberries, blueberries, peaches, etc. [pg. 42]).

Granulated Flavor

INGREDIENTS:
- ¾ cup cane sugar
- 1 cup milk
- 2 cups heavy whipping cream
- 2 Tablespoons flavor powder (choose one below):
    - Ground Cinnamon
    - Espresso Instant Coffee

STEPS:
1. Stir flavor powder into milk and microwave until warm, about 1 minute. After heating, stir again to combine flavor powder into milk.
2. Whisk sugar in the warm milk mixture.
3. Add heavy cream to milk mixture and stir.
4. Chill, churn, and set.

HERE'S THE SCOOP:

This recipe is best used for a grainy cinnamon or smooth coffee flavor. After chilling, there's usually a "skin" on the mixture. You can stir it back in or just pour it straight into the churning vessel, as it doesn't make much of a difference.

We toyed with trying to make a "Mexican Hot Chocolate" recipe. It included some nutmeg and cayenne pepper to add some spice to the ice cream. Unfortunately, the dairy in the recipe negated most—if not all—of the capsaicin. If we were to try making a spicy ice cream recipe again, we'd likely use this recipe with cayenne pepper or ground white pepper.

 It might tempt you to try a powdered flavor like Kool-Aid or Tang. This it will have the same chalky and artificial taste that you'd get if you used Mio in the Extract recipe. Similarly, don't attempt to use powdered cocoa for this base, as there is a much better chocolate recipe later in this chapter (*see: Chocolate [pg. 30]*).

Juice Sorbet

INGREDIENTS:
- 1 ¼ cup cane sugar
- 1 cup water
- 2 pounds fresh (rinsed) or frozen (thawed) fruit, (choose one below):
  - Raspberries
  - Blackberries
  - Blueberries
  - Strawberries, trimmed and diced
  - Cherries, pitted
  - Cranberries
  - Kiwi, peeled and diced
  - Dragon fruit, peeled and diced

STEPS:
1. Heat water and sugar in large saucepan over high heat until dissolved and just simmering.
2. Once sugar mixture is dissolved and boiling, add fruit and boil for 10 minutes or until fruit is soft.
3. Off the heat, mash thoroughly with a potato

masher.

4. Strain the mixture to remove skins and seeds, pressing and scraping the mixture against the strainer to get the most juice out of it as possible.
5. Chill, churn, and set.

Variations:
- Sherbet
  - Additional Ingredients:
    - ½ cup milk
    - ½ cup heavy whipping cream
    - **Subtract:** 8 ounces of fruit
  - Additional Steps:
    - Before churning, mix in milk and heavy cream and stir to combine.
- Chocolate-covered Fruit
  - Additional Ingredients:
    - 1 pack instant chocolate or white chocolate pudding mix
    - ½ cup milk
    - ½ cup heavy whipping cream
    - **Subtract:** 8 ounces of fruit
  - Additional Steps:
    - Before churning, mix in milk and heavy cream and stir to combine.
    - Stir in pack of pudding mix and immediately pour into the ice cream maker.

Here's the Scoop:
You can choose to use less fruit in this recipe, but it makes less volume. To remedy this, you can churn at a faster setting to whip more air into the mixture, creating a

Stop Screaming!

fluffy mousse that fills a full quart container. Alternatively, adding more water or dairy (as per the variations) will increase the volume of this base.

The key to distinguishing which fruit to use for this recipe when compared with the next sorbet recipe is whether you can blend the boiled fruit into a pulp. Most of the fruits in this recipe have hard seeds (i.e., blackberries or cherries) or unappetizing skins that need to be strained. For some of the softer seed fruits (i.e., strawberries or kiwis), you can add some of the seedy pulp into the base to add texture. It doesn't matter if you use fresh or frozen fruit, as long as you let the frozen fruit thaw before boiling it.

If your sorbet isn't quite flavorful by itself, you can add 1 to 2 Tablespoons of lemon juice just before churning to enhance the flavor. Be careful, though, as one of our early failures was trying to make a blueberry compote recipe. Something went wrong when we made it and the recipe curdled. We took one bite and gave up. Normally, we suffer through failed recipes and eat what we have made. This was one of the two recipes we rinsed down the sink as immediately as possible. Never again.

For those who are curious, the recipes in this cookbook labeled as sorbet are not to be confused with sherbet. Sorbet is dairy free and made primarily with fruit. Sherbet can also be made with fruit but contains milk. For anyone lactose intolerant, a sorbet is a perfect dessert! To make any of these sorbets into sherbets, follow the Sherbet variation and add ½ cup milk and ½ cup heavy cream to the mixture and stir before churning.

In terms of the chocolate-covered fruit variation, be aware that adding the chocolate pudding will make a lot of ice cream. Reducing the amount of fruit you use should help with this volume issue. Also, we usually use the Hershey's brand chocolate pudding (both regular and white chocolate), as the store brand packs have a chalky texture. **DO NOT USE SUGAR FREE**. The best fruits to use for this variation are blackberry, raspberry, and strawberry.

PULP SORBET

INGREDIENTS:
- 1 ¼ cup cane sugar
- 1 cup water
- Pinch of salt
- 2 pounds fresh (rinsed) or frozen (thawed) fruit, peeled and diced (choose one below):
    - Mango
    - Peach
    - Nectarine
    - Rhubarb
    - Banana
    - Pineapple
    - Cantaloupe
    - Honeydew
    - Watermelon (Seedless)
- 4 Tablespoons alcohol (choose one below):
    - Rum
    - Tequila
    - Vodka
    - Whiskey
    - Bourbon
    - Brandy
    - Triple sec

STEPS:
1. Heat water, sugar, and salt in large saucepan over high heat until dissolved and just simmering.

2. Once the sugar mixture is dissolved and boiling, add fruit and boil for 10 minutes or until it has the consistency of chunky mush.
3. Off the heat, let cool for 15 minutes.
4. Add alcohol.
5. Pour mixture in blender or food processor and blend until completely smooth. Alternatively, use an immersion blender in the saucepan to get the same result.
6. Chill, churn, and set.

VARIATIONS:

- Sherbet
  - Additional Ingredients:
    - ½ cup milk
    - ½ cup heavy whipping cream
    - **SUBTRACT:** 8 ounces of fruit
  - Additional Steps:
    - Before churning, mix in milk and heavy cream and stir to combine.
- Margarita/Daiquirí
  - Additional Ingredients:
    - 3 Tablespoons citrus juice
      - Lemon
      - Lime
      - Orange
      - Lemon-Lime Soda
  - Additional Steps:
    - Include citrus juice when adding alcohol.

HERE'S THE SCOOP:

The smoothness of this sorbet lies in its alcohol content. Notice that 4 Tablespoons of total alcohol is the best amount to ensure the mixture freezes. We've also found that the more fibrous sorbets benefit from the alcohol content. Otherwise, they trap the moisture and freeze hard into ice cubes. Experiment with what alcohols work best for which fruits. Rum is probably the most consistent across all fruit options, but a smoky whisky can go great with peach or nectarine.

Because this recipe uses alcohol, you can add 3 Tablespoons of citrus juice to arrive at a margarita or daiquirí flavoring. You might be tempted to make a pina colada sherbet by adding a ½ cup of coconut milk to a pineapple base. Just know that most sherbets work because of the fat content in the milk, so it might not turn out. This is also on top of the fact that the pineapple version of this recipe needs a lot of blending to get completely smooth.

You might notice an odd ingredient in this recipe: rhubarb. The Weilert family has a long history with rhubarb. We're a little like Bubba from *Forrest Gump*, except with rhubarb instead of shrimp. We have great recipes for rhubarb cobblers, rhubarb jams, and (as you've seen here) rhubarb sorbet. This tart treat is popular among my family mostly because it grows so well in Colorado's soil and climate.

We're not entirely sure how we grow such great rhubarb. As far as we can tell, if you plant a rhubarb next to your house and then do nothing other than pick the stalks when they're ready, it'll grow like a weed. There's usually a downspout nearby to water it regularly when it rains. I'm of the opinion that the residual heat and protection from

the house causes the rhubarb to thrive. Of course, we jok-
ingly think that rhubarb flourishes because it's sucking
away the minerals from the foundation of the house. If the
corner of my house ever collapses, it'll be the first thing I'll
suspect.

For the rhubarb sorbet, use the pink stalks where you
can. If you use all pink stalks, the result is a pretty pink
color. If you use the green stalks, it will still taste the same,
but the color will look like snot. To make it look pinker,
you can use about 9 drops of red food coloring in the boiling stage of this recipe to counteract the green color.

Most recipes up to this point have
been relatively simple. Now we're going to get a little advanced. The reason
these next few bases can be some of
the trickier recipes to make is mostly
because they require tempering eggs.
The reason we pour the hot milk mixture into the whisked egg yolks is because if we pour the eggs into the hot
milk, it may be too hot and will curdle.
A curdled base is unrecoverable, as
you're left with scrambled eggs in your ice cream. It might
take a little practice, but the key is to keep scraping the bottom of your pan, pour the hot milk mixture along the side
of the bowl with the egg yolks in it, and to pay close atten-
tion to the thermometer as you stir.

CAKE BATTER

INGREDIENTS:

- ¾ cup cane sugar
- 1 cup milk
- 2 cups heavy whipping cream
- 1 egg yolk
- 1 Tablespoon unsalted butter
- 1 cup cake mix (choose one below):
    - Yellow Cake
    - Spice Cake
    - Red Velvet
    - Pancake Mix

STEPS:

1. Whisk egg yolk in medium bowl.
2. In a saucepan or double boiler, heat milk and sugar on medium heat until just simmering, about 150° F.
3. Slowly pour half of the hot milk mixture into egg yolks, tempering the eggs.
4. Add butter to the remaining hot milk mixture.
5. Pour tempered mixture back into saucepan or double boiler and stir, scraping the bottom until a thermometer reads 170° F.
6. Remove from heat and let mixture set in a clean bowl for 5 minutes.
7. Sprinkle cake mix over the surface of the mixture, allowing the butter to absorb into the cake mix.
8. Add heavy whipping cream and stir until mixture is smooth.
9. Chill, churn, and set.

Stop Screaming!

Here's the Scoop:

While the result is one of the richest bases in this chapter, it may freeze harder than you expect. Place the container in the microwave for 15 seconds to soften it as needed before serving. Alternatively, add a few Tablespoons of grain alcohol (no more than 4) right before churning. The alcohol lowers the freezing temperature, so the ice cream stays softer, resulting in a smoother base that's easier to scoop.

Even though Red Velvet is basically a chocolate cake, you can find a much better chocolate base in the last recipe of this chapter [*pg. 30*]. You don't need to do a Devil's Food Cake version of this base.

Citrus Custard

Ingredients:

- ¾ cup cane sugar
- 1 cup milk
- 2 cups heavy whipping cream
- 6 egg yolks
- 4 teaspoons citrus zest
- ⅓ cup fresh citrus juice (choose one below):
  - o 2 medium lemons
  - o 3 large limes
  - o 1 large orange
  - o 1 large grapefruit

Steps:

1. Whisk egg yolks in medium bowl.
2. Mix milk, sugar, zest, and heavy cream in a double boiler or saucepan on medium heat until just simmering, about 150° F.

3. Slowly pour half of the hot milk mixture into egg yolks, tempering the eggs.
4. Pour tempered mixture back into double boiler or saucepan and stir, scraping the bottom until a thermometer reads 170° F.
5. Remove from heat and let cool for 15 minutes.
6. Add fresh citrus juice and strain mixture into clean bowl.
7. Chill, churn, and set.

HERE'S THE SCOOP:

For the oranges, try to use ones with the most flavorful juices (i.e., Valencia, blood, and navel oranges). Otherwise, the flavor can be rather faint and underwhelming.

To add a little texture to this base, you can save up to a teaspoon of zest to mix in after straining. Don't overdo it, though, as too much zest can make the ice cream taste waxy.

If you're using the Kitchen-Aid for your ice cream vessel, the juicing attachment works wonders for quickly juicing the citrus. Just make sure you strain the pulp and seeds from the juice before adding it to the recipe.

My wife's family has a dessert they only serve during birthdays called Darn Good. They changed its original name of Damn Good for the sake of the children. This lemon custard dessert was one inspiration for this recipe, which includes a meringue mix-in (*see: Meringue* [*pg. 40*]). As a tradition, they made Darn Good with one lemon seed left in for good luck. Whoever took a bite and found the seed was granted good luck for the next year. You can add a lemon seed to this base right before chilling to create the same effect.

CHOCOLATE

INGREDIENTS:
- ¾ cup cane sugar
- 1 cup milk
- 2 cups heavy whipping cream
- 4 egg yolks
- 4 ounces chocolate (choose one below):
    - Semisweet baker's chocolate (~56% cacao)
    - White chocolate

STEPS:
1. Whisk egg yolks in medium bowl.
2. In a saucepan, heat milk and sugar on medium heat until just simmering, about 150° F.
3. Slowly pour half of the hot milk mixture into egg yolks, tempering the eggs.
4. Pour tempered mixture back into saucepan and stir, scraping the bottom until a thermometer reads 170° F.
5. Chop or break chocolate into small pieces and add to the top pan of a double boiler on medium high heat.
6. Slowly add heavy whipping cream to the partially melted chocolate and allow the chocolate to continue to melt.
7. Once the chocolate is smooth, pour the chocolate into a clean bowl.
8. Strain the tempered mixture into the same bowl as the chocolate and mix well.
9. Chill, churn, and set.

HERE'S THE SCOOP:

Before churning, be sure to mix the chocolate thoroughly again, as it will have a thick "crust" that solidified during the chilling process.

You may think you can create a dark chocolate base by substituting the semisweet baker's chocolate with dark baker's chocolate. However, know that the addition of milk and cream will automatically make your ice cream into a milk chocolate base. Alternatively, try using white chocolate if you want to mix this recipe up a little.

One of our earliest mistakes was our attempt at making chocolate ice cream with Hershey's chocolate bars instead of baker's chocolate. We were high off our initial success with vanilla, so we figured why not just repeat the process and add some chocolate to make chocolate ice cream? Unfortunately, the resulting ice cream was chalky and gross.

Most chocolate bars have some preservatives in them. These preservatives help to keep the chocolate tasting fresh and consistent over long amounts of time. However, these preservatives come to the forefront of the palate when melted down. If you want the "correct" chocolate for a chocolate base, use the bars found in the baking aisle and not the candy aisle.

CHAPTER 3: MIX-INS

A nyone who has been a customer of Cold Stone Cream-ery will know how mix-ins work. If the base of an ice cream is its foundation, the mix-ins are the building blocks for truly complex flavors and textures. While each base can stand on its own, a mix-in is an addition that enhances the ice cream.

Growing up, I tried many mix-in combinations at Cold Stone. I learned quickly that some mix-ins just don't work. Gummy bears and marshmallows were nice and chewy at room temperature. However, when mixed into ice cream, they turned into little rock-hard chunks that were difficult to chew. In basic science terms, the elasticity of these mix-ins decreases, which makes them stiffer. The challenge for chewy mix-ins is to figure out how to make them keep their chewiness in the ice cream.

When dealing with mix-ins, you need to understand two realities:

1. **Something that's chewy at room temperature will be rock hard when frozen.**
2. **Thermodynamics wants everything to be at the same temperature.**

I've already covered the first reality, but the second reality is why we suggest freezing these mix-ins prior to their inclusion in the churning process. For example, if you have a chunk of crushed Oreo cookie that you want to mix into a vanilla base, if it's at room temperature, the chilled vanilla base will try to cool it down. This causes the Oreo to absorb the base and become soggy. However, if you already froze the Oreo, the mix-in will be the one trying to cool down the base. Since the base is actively being chilled in the ice cream maker vessel, this is the thermodynamic direction you want the process to go. Alternatively, the later you introduce a mix-in to a base, the less time it has to alter the thermodynamics of the mixture. Just be sure you don't add it too late when the base is close to being set, otherwise you might break your ice cream maker.

Because you can add many of these mix-ins to different bases, it's important to know how to make them in isolation. As with the previous chapter, I will try to arrange these mix-ins with increasing levels of complexity. We'll go over the combined recipes of the bases and mix-ins in the next chapter, but you can also mix and match mix-ins and bases to create your own unique flavors.

The goal is to have a mix-in that doesn't completely overwhelm a base, but enhances it through an additional flavor or texture. Ideally, you'll want ¼ to ½ of a cup of an individual mix-in, with the pieces of the mix-in no larger than ½-inch in diameter. Some of these recipes make more than a ½ cup and you can freeze the remaining mix-in to use later or add more to the base per your preferences.

Since mix-ins add a lot of volume to a recipe, be sure that you add no more than three mix-ins into a base. Be sure to check with your ice cream maker's manufacturer's instructions to determine the size limit of the mix-ins, both in diameter and in volume.

A repeated warning about mix-ins: make sure your chunks are small enough! Anecdotally, bigger chunks are more likely to get caught in the paddle and cause problems. Since many mix-ins require freezing before incorporating into the base, the frozen chunks are quite hard. Unfortunately, the combination of frozen mix-in caught in the paddle caused the piece of the ice cream maker attachment that interfaces with our Kitchen-Aid mixer to break. This was a plastic piece and was bound to have a weak spot or two. However, after buying a new ice cream maker attachment—which was cheaper than getting a new plastic piece—we noticed it had changed design in the six years since they made our first one. Perhaps this design change was because others had the same problem.

If you want larger mix-in chunks or your ice cream maker is limited by the size or volume, you can fold them in as the ice cream is being moved to the container for freezing. I recommend giving the base a couple of folding twists after churning, regardless.

Chips

Ingredients:
- ⅓ cup chips (choose one below):
  - Mini semisweet chocolate chips
  - Mini M&M's
  - Rainbow sprinkles

Steps:
1. As the base is being churned, add chips ¾ of the way through the process.

Here's the Scoop:
This is probably the easiest mix-in to handle. Even the mini semisweet chocolate chips are thick enough that they won't completely dissolve in the base. Be sure to get the

mini-sized chocolate chips or M&M's, as anything bigger gets too hard to bite into when you freeze the base. Chilling the sprinkles ahead of time will also keep their dyes from leeching into the base as it finishes churning.

CANDY

INGREDIENTS:
- 20 crushed candies, unwrapped [~100 grams] (choose one below):
  o Werther's Originals Caramels
  o Lemon
  o Peppermint
  o Butterscotch
  o Cinnamon
  o Blue Raspberry
  o Heath Bars

STEPS:
1. Crush candies into ½-inch pieces. Keeping them in their individual wrappers helps keep the pieces consolidated.
2. As the base is being churned, add crushed candies ¼ of the way through the process.

HERE'S THE SCOOP:
Sometimes, having remnants of the candies used for a base is a great way to introduce a crunchy texture to your ice cream. You don't need to freeze these crushed pieces since they don't dissolve that much into the base. Some ideal candies for this method are peppermints and lemon drops. As with the Candy base [*pg. 16*], be careful to not use any candies with waxy consistencies, like jellybeans, lic-

orice, or Lemonheads. Similarly, as noted in the introduction to this chapter, avoid chewy candies if you don't want them to harden in the base.

Cookie

Ingredients:
- 1 ½ cups cookies—~10 cookies, 1 ¾" diameter (choose one below):
  - o Oreos
  - o Chocolate Chip
  - o Nilla Wafers
  - o Snickerdoodles
  - o Girl Scout Thin Mints
  - o Keebler Grasshoppers
  - o Gingersnaps

Steps:
1. Using a meat tenderizer and a small bowl, crush batches of 3-4 cookies until there are no pieces larger than ½-inch (about marble sized).
2. Store crushed cookie bits in sealed container in freezer until ready to churn the base.
3. As the base is being churned, add crushed cookies ½ of the way through the process. Because of the chilled nature of this mix-in, it may reduce the churning time.

Here's the Scoop:
Our go to for this mix-in is Oreo cookies. Considering all the Oreo flavors that exist nowadays, this can provide a variety of interesting flavors for mix-ins. We use roughly one sleeve of cookies for this mix-in and eat the rest. One thing to consider is how early to add the cookies during the

churning process. Too early, and the cookies create enough crumbs to make the ice cream look like roadside slush after a snowstorm[5].

NUTS

INGREDIENTS:
- ¼ cup pre-chopped nuts of ½-inch size (choose one below):
    o Almonds
    o Walnuts
    o Pecans
    o Peanuts

STEPS:
1. As the base is being churned, add nuts ¾ of the way through the process.

HERE'S THE SCOOP:

Both my wife and I are allergic to most nuts, but we know that some ice cream recipes call for this ingredient. Fortunately, we aren't as allergic to almonds, so we did test to make sure this mix-in works as intended.

We found that the bag of "slivers" works best for this mix-in if you want to just dump in ¼ cup of nuts. However, if you have whole nuts or the pre-chopped nuts have large chunks, use a knife or kitchen shears to chop them into ½-inch pieces. Sift out any dust and smaller particles before mixing into the base. Raw or toasted nuts work fine for this mix-in, just don't pick the ones with extra salt as that may affect the taste of the ice cream overall.

---

[5] The ice cream still tastes good, though.

GRAHAM CRACKER

INGREDIENTS:
- 2 sheets of graham crackers
- 1 ½ Tablespoons unsalted butter, melted

STEPS:
1. Crush graham crackers into crumbs.
2. Combine graham cracker crumbs and butter in a bowl or container, stirring until they form ½-inch marble sized chunks.
3. Let cool in freezer.
4. Before churning the base, break apart any pieces that froze together while in the freezer.
5. As the base is being churned, add graham crackers ¾ of the way through the process.

HERE'S THE SCOOP:
This mix-in is key to the cheesecake recipes [*pg. 58*]. Adding this mix-in and a fruit mix-in is almost the same as having cheesecake! It can also be used as a pie crust stand-in for recipes that emulate the pie experience.

BROWNIE

INGREDIENTS:
- 1 box brownie mix
    - 1 egg
    - ⅓ cup vegetable oil
    - ⅓ cup water

STEPS:
1. Prepare brownies as instructed on the box and undercook in a 9" x 13" pan by 2 minutes.

2. After cutting off and removing the edges from the pan, cube a quarter of the batch of brownies into ½-inch pieces, about 20 pieces.
3. Freeze in an air-tight container.
4. As the base is being churned, add brownie bits ½ of the way through the process.

VARIATION:

- Cookie Dough
    - o Additional Ingredients:
        - **REPLACE:** Brownie bits with pre-made bits of cookie dough
    - o Additional Steps:
        - Cut cookie dough into smaller pieces (roughly ½-inch diameter).

HERE'S THE SCOOP:

A pan of brownies will produce enough for four batches of brownie mix-ins. This produces a large amount of volume for a mix-in, so be sure to use a larger container when freezing. Preparing the brownies according to the "fudge style" helps to create the density of brownies desired for this mix-in's consistency. Fortunately, the oil in this recipe, combined with under-cooking the brownies, makes these brownie chunks nice and chewy in the final product.

Similarly, using a tray of pre-made cookie dough (not the tube) guarantees the consistency of the cookie dough bits. This mix-in is all about the chewy mouth feel, so slightly larger pieces aren't a problem here. Chocolate chip cookie dough is the traditional version of this mix-in, but feel free to try other flavors from your grocery store's dairy section.

MERINGUE

INGREDIENTS:
- ⅓ cup cane sugar
- 2 egg whites
- ¼ teaspoon salt

STEPS:
1. Preheat oven to 270° F.
2. Combine ingredients and whisk until stiff peaks begin to form.
3. Spread meringue ½-inch thick on a sheet of parchment paper held on a baking sheet.
4. Place in the oven and let cook for one hour.
5. Without opening the oven, turn the oven off and let the meringue set for an additional hour.
6. Remove meringue from the oven and break into ½-inch, marble-sized pieces.
7. Store meringue pieces in freezer for at least 2 hours.
8. As the base is being churned, add meringue ¾ of the way through the process.

VARIATION:
- Marshmallow
  - Additional Ingredients:
    - **REPLACE:** ⅓ cup sugar with ⅓ cup marshmallow crème
  - Additional Steps:
    - Use an eggbeater instead of a whisk to fully incorporate the marshmallow crème into the eggs.

HERE'S THE SCOOP:

Meringue is quite simple to make and becomes slightly chewier when mixed into an ice cream base because of its absorption of some of the base's moisture. For a mix-in that's just whipped air, meringue adds just enough texture to a base to make things interesting.

It is challenging to get a true marshmallow mix-in due to the stickiness of marshmallow crème and the hardness of frozen mini marshmallows. However, using this meringue recipe with marshmallow crème replacing the sugar is a neat trick to emulate the chewiness and taste of marshmallows.

BROWN SUGAR

INGREDIENTS:

- 1 cup light brown sugar
- 1 to 2 teaspoons water

STEPS:

1. Using a saucepan, warm the brown sugar and water on medium heat, stirring regularly with a wooden spoon until it just turns into liquid. Add 1 to 2 more teaspoons of water if your brown sugar is particularly dry.
2. Quickly pour melted brown sugar onto parchment paper on a baking sheet.
3. Let cool for 30 minutes.
4. Break caramelized sugar into ½-inch pieces and store in an air-tight container in freezer before churning. This might require kitchen shears.
5. As the base is being churned, add brown sugar ¾ of the way through the process.

Stop Screaming!

Here's the Scoop:

This mix-in is for the Crème Brûlée recipe [*pg. 53*] but you can add it to any other recipe for a strudel-like texture and taste. Originally, we made this mix-in by putting brown sugar on a pan and broiling it in the oven for a few minutes to get that melted texture. After at least two instances of the brown sugar catching fire using this technique, one of our testers suggested this much safer alternative.

Fruit

Ingredients:

- 1 ½ cup fruit, rinsed, peeled, pitted, and chopped into roughly ½-inch pieces (choose one below):
    - Strawberries
    - Apples
    - Peaches
    - Nectarines
    - Cherries
    - Raisins
    - Dried Cranberries
    - Carrots
- ¼ cup granulated cane sugar or brown sugar
- ¼ cup alcohol, as needed (choose one below):
    - Vodka (non-flavored or flavored)
    - Whiskey (non-flavored or flavored)
    - Bourbon (non-flavored or flavored)
    - Brandy (non-flavored or flavored)
    - Rum
    - Flavored liqueurs

Steps:

1. Mix fruit with granulated sugar and let sit for 20 minutes.
2. Preheat oven to 425° F.
3. Drain fruit of any excess liquid.
4. Spread a layer of sugared fruit on parchment paper on a baking sheet.
5. Roast fruit in oven on the top rack for 10 minutes and let cool. Drain excess liquid.
6. If needed, put roasted fruit in a bowl and pour alcohol into the bowl to just cover the fruit.
7. Soak fruit in alcohol in refrigerator for 2 to 4 hours.
8. Strain fruit from alcohol and keep in refrigerator in an air-tight container until base is ready for churning.
9. As the base is being churned, add fruit ½ of the way through the process.

Here's the Scoop:

Fruit can be a tricky mix-in mostly because of its water content. If you've ever eaten frozen fruit from the frozen section at the grocery store, you'll know that most fruit freezes in the same way that ice cubes do. The water in this fruit is just an ice cube surrounded by fruit if it isn't removed or replaced before mixing with the base[6].

There are three methods to reduce the amount of moisture content in the fruit used for mix-ins. This recipe covers all three, and sometimes you will only need the first two. Coating fruit in sugar allows the sugar to extract the latent moisture from the fruit. Roasting the fruit in the oven allows excess moisture to evaporate. Soaking fruit in

---

[6] Recall the first reality of mix-ins: something chewy at room temperature will be rock hard when frozen.

alcohol replaces the water with alcohol—which, if you recall from the bases with alcohol, doesn't freeze.

You may use frozen fruit for this mix-in, being sure to thaw it completely at room temperature before applying the moisture-reducing techniques covered here.

The fruit mix-in works best with chunks of fruit. Do not use berries with harder seeds (i.e., blackberries, blueberries, and raspberries). It is difficult, if not impossible, to remove the seeds from these fruits without also making the fruit into a pulpy paste. I learned this lesson when I attempted a triple berry cheesecake recipe with strawberries, blueberries, and blackberries. It was hard to enjoy the flavor of the ice cream when my teeth kept hitting the blackberry seeds.

Different fruits will have different moisture contents and sometimes do not need all three methods prior to including in a recipe. The following list gives some examples of what to do for a variety of fruit:

- **STRAWBERRIES:** Coating in sugar and roasting in the oven is more than enough.
- **APPLES:** 1 large apple = 1 ½ cups. Be sure to peel the apples before chopping. Depending on your recipe, you can soak these in a basic grain alcohol (e.g., vodka) or a brandy (apple-flavored brandy can also enhance the flavor).
- **PEACHES:** 1 large peach = 1 cup. Firm peaches are easier to chop into pieces. Substitute half the granulated sugar with brown sugar and soak in whiskey (a peach-flavored whiskey enhances the flavor).
- **CHERRIES:** 1 pound bag = 2 cups. After removing the seed and pit, cut each cherry into eighths. Soaking these in cherry liqueur can make the flavor really pop but will also bring the alcohol taste to the

forefront of the palate. Alternatively, Maraschino cherries work without any modifications.

- **RAISINS:** Adding a little cinnamon and/or nutmeg to the sugar helps bring out a deeper flavor profile here. You can skip the roasting stage for this fruit since they already have minimal moisture. You only need ¾ cup of raisins instead of the 1 ½ cups this mix-in calls for since the dehydration stage was already performed.
- **DRIED CRANBERRIES:** Similar to raisins, you don't need to roast them due to them already being dried. Soak in alcohol to re-hydrate and you're good to go. Should work for other dried fruits as well.
- **CARROTS:** 2 large carrots = 1 ½ cups. Shredded carrots work best for this, considering they're only used in the Carrot Cake recipe for texture (*see: Carrot Cake [pg. 65]*). Use brown sugar instead of cane sugar, but only half of the alcohol (vodka is recommended). Carrots are notorious for holding and absorbing moisture, so you might find that the alcohol overwhelms the flavor here.

S'MORES

INGREDIENTS:
- 4 ounces chocolate (choose one below):
    o Baker's semisweet chocolate
    o Chocolate chips (dark chocolate or milk chocolate)
- 8 sheets graham crackers broken into square pieces
- 13-ounce container marshmallow creme

Stop Screaming!

Steps:

1. Preheat oven to 500° F on the broil setting.
2. Break graham cracker sheets into square pieces.
3. Spread a thin layer of marshmallow crème on one graham cracker square, being sure to cover the entire graham cracker with marshmallow crème. Then, spread a thicker layer of marshmallow paste on another graham cracker square (about ½-inch thick). Put the first graham cracker square on top of the marshmallow crème of the second one with the thin layer of marshmallow crème up. Repeat until you've used all the graham cracker squares.
4. Place marshmallow'd graham cracker sandwiches on parchment paper on a baking sheet. Ensure the thin layer of marshmallow crème is facing upward.
5. Roast in oven on the top rack, watching carefully for smoke. Singe the top layers of the marshmallow and a bit of the graham cracker. About 2 minutes.
6. Remove baking sheet from oven and flip graham crackers over so the marshmallow side is down on the parchment paper.
7. Turn the oven off.
8. Distribute ½ ounce of chocolate on each of the crackers and let them melt. Return to the warm oven for 2 minutes if needed.
9. Using a butter-knife, spread the melted chocolate across the entire surface of the graham crackers.
10. Let cool until chocolate is completely set before breaking into ½-inch pieces (break through the chocolate side).
11. Chill s'more pieces in an air-tight container in the freezer before churning.

46

HERE'S THE SCOOP:

The singed marshmallow and graham cracker is the source of the campfire flavor. This recipe will make a double batch of s'more pieces to be used as a mix-in, so be sure to not dump everything in the base when churning it.

SYRUP SWIRL

INGREDIENTS:

- ¼ cup light corn syrup
- ¼ cup of flavored syrup (choose one below):
    - Maraschino Cherry[7]
    - Honey[8]
    - Maple Syrup
    - Caramel Syrup
    - Marshmallow Syrup
    - Soda

STEPS:

1. Combine flavored syrup and light corn syrup in a small saucepan.
2. Cook on medium heat until the syrup thickens and reduces by about half. This happens when at least two of three things occur:
    i. Bubbles from the boiling syrup become larger (~1-2 inches in diameter) and don't readily pop.
    ii. A candy thermometer reads at least 205° F. You may have to tilt the syrup to the side of the pan to get an accurate reading.
    iii. Skin forms on the surface of the syrup.

---

[7] Use ½ cup of this ingredient—no light corn syrup needed.
[8] No need to add light corn syrup to this ingredient, use as is.

3. Let the syrup cool for 2 minutes.

4. Pour reduced syrup into a sealable baggie and store in the refrigerator in a small bowl or mug. When chilled, it should feel like gel.

5. After churning the base, scoop it into the container being used for freezing.

6. Cut a corner off the sealable baggie and squeeze the reduced syrup into the freezing container.

7. Using a butter-knife, stab and swirl through the layer of syrup so that it can "drain" into the base.

HERE'S THE SCOOP:

The trick with this mix-in is to evaporate enough of the water from the syrup so that it doesn't just dissolve into the base as it's being chilled. This mix-in also frequently sinks to the bottom of the container, so be sure that the base isn't runny before adding the syrup on top.

There are a variety of flavors you can use for this mix-in. Originally, we used the syrup from a 10-ounce jar of maraschino cherries, so it's our baseline for this mix-in. You can also use maple syrup, soda, or any of the flavored syrups (like caramel) that are found in the coffee section of your grocery store.

Here are tips for the following flavors:

- **MARASCHINO CHERRY:** The original syrup swirl mix-in. If you need a baseline for the other syrups in terms of viscosity or consistency, this is the syrup to use. No additional corn syrup is needed.

- **HONEY:** This syrup swirl mix-in requires no additional reduction. Use ¼ cup instead of ½ cup because there is no need to reduce it.

- **MAPLE SYRUP:** If you're using pure maple syrup, you'll want to add the light corn syrup for stability.

Since many maple syrups are mostly just corn syrup, you can get away with just reducing ½ cup of this ingredient without additional corn syrup.

Be aware that this mix-in can be very finnicky. Over-reducing the syrup will create a rock-hard chunk in the ice cream while under-reducing the syrup will cause it to sink to the bottom of the base. To solve over-reducing, let the baggie return to room temperature, add a Tablespoon of the original flavor into the baggie, then put back in the refrigerator. Repeat as needed. To solve under-reducing, merely return to the saucepan and simmer until desired consistency is reached. Don't feel bad if you can't get this right after a few tries—this is the most advanced recipe in this book.

CHAPTER 4: COMBINATIONS

N ow that you know how to make the bases and mix-ins, it's time to put everything together and start making full recipes! This is the portion of the book where you can be experimental. Mix and match bases with mix-ins and see if you like the result.

Sometimes, even the combinations you think would work don't. Case in point: we made a raspberry/blackberry sorbet with an Oreo mix-in because I saw something similar at the grocery store. The sorbet flavor was too powerful for the cookie mix-in. I didn't quite get the result I was looking for. It was still worth it to experiment, though.

I've included the recipes that work for us below as a jumping-off point for you to explore different combinations. I have noted bases and mix-ins with variations in parentheses. The recipes below are arranged based on the order of the bases in Chapter 2, followed by the order of mix-ins in Chapter 3.

Any modifications to the base or mix-in will have annotations in these recipes. Sometimes a recipe requires tweaks from a few different techniques learned in the last two chapters in order to work.

Remember: individual mix-ins should be about ¼ to ½ cup in volume. Adding two or more mix-ins will probably require you to use the larger containers for setting/storing in your freezer. If the mix-in chunks are too big, fold them into the base while in the ice cream vessel before scooping into the freezing container.

COOKIES & CREAM

BASE:
Extract (Vanilla) [*pg. 13*]
MIX-IN:
10 Cookie (Oreo) [*pg. 36*]
MODIFICATIONS:
None.

HERE'S THE SCOOP:
We've found Oreos to be the best cookie for this ice cream, but try your favorites to see if anything else works better.

CHOCOLATE CHIP COOKIE DOUGH

BASE:
Extract (Vanilla) [*pg. 13*]
MIX-IN:
⅙ cup Chips (Chocolate Chips) [*pg. 34*]
20 Brownie (Cookie Dough: Chocolate Chip) [*pg. 39*]
MODIFICATIONS:
Add ½ teaspoon of salt to the Vanilla base. Use half the volume of Chocolate Chips (⅙ cup), but also use larger chips.

HERE'S THE SCOOP:
The extra salt in the base highlights the saltiness in the Cookie Dough mix-in. The additional Chocolate Chip mix-in can be left out entirely if desired, but it adds a good crunch outside the chewy Cookie Dough pieces.

Rum Raisin

Base:
Extract (Vanilla) [*pg. 13*]
Mix-in:
¾ cup Fruit (Raisin) [*pg. 42*]
Modifications:
Use ¾ cup of raisins as the Fruit mix-in with rum as the soaking alcohol. Add ½ teaspoon nutmeg and ½ teaspoon cinnamon to the sugar.

Here's the Scoop:
You do not need to bake the raisins since they already have minimal moisture in them, and the alcohol soak is all that's needed to ensure they remain chewy in the base.

Harvest Pie

Base:
Extract (Vanilla) [*pg. 13*]
Mix-in:
¼ cup Graham Cracker [*pg. 38*]
1 ½ cup Fruit (Apple, Golden Raisins, and Dried Cranberries) [*pg. 42*]
Modifications:
Use ¼ cup dried cranberries, 1 cup golden delicious apples (~1 large apple), and ¼ cup golden raisins for the Fruit mix-in. Add 1 ½ teaspoon ground cinnamon and ½ teaspoon nutmeg to the sugar used for roasting the apples. Do not roast the cranberries and raisins. Soak all fruits in

whiskey, being sure to include as much of the roasted cinnamon and nutmeg as possible.

HERE'S THE SCOOP:

Harvest Pie is a favorite holiday recipe in my family. Every time we add the spices to the fruits, the entire house smells spectacular. This recipe tries to recreate that experience by including all the fruits involved in the filling and adding the spices to the roasting process.

CRÈME BRÛLÉE

BASE:
Extract (Vanilla) [*pg. 13*]
MIX-IN:
½ cup Brown Sugar [*pg. 41*]
MODIFICATIONS:
None.

HERE'S THE SCOOP:

The trick for this one is getting the caramelized brown sugar into the base without dissolving too much. If your Brown Sugar mix-in is too smooth, fold in a teaspoon of un-melted brown sugar when you scoop this base into the freezing container. This helps emulate the gritty texture.

FRUIT & CREAM

BASE:
Extract (Vanilla) [*pg. 13*]
MIX-IN:
1 ½ cup Fruit (Strawberries or Peaches) [*pg. 42*]

Stop Screaming!

MODIFICATIONS:

If desired, substitute ½ cup of milk with an additional ½ cup of heavy whipping cream for the Vanilla base.

HERE'S THE SCOOP:

Sometimes, the simplest ice creams are the best. Vanilla, chocolate, and strawberry are basic enough flavors that any amateur homemade ice cream cook like yourself should be able to create. Adding extra cream in the base helps to emulate the berries and cream or peaches and cream flavor profile.

CHRISTMAS IN JULY

BASE:

Extract (Vanilla or Mint) [*pg. 13*]

MIX-IN:

20 Candy (Peppermint) [*pg. 35*]

MODIFICATIONS:

Use peppermint candy canes or peppermint discs for the Candy mix-in, including chunks no larger than ¼ the size of a peppermint disc.

HERE'S THE SCOOP:

While you rarely want the candy to dissolve into the base, peppermint candy is a strong enough flavor that its addition to the base is desirable here. With larger chunks included, there's still that bit of candy crunch that's satisfying in a Vanilla base. Alternatively, for extreme effect, you can use a Mint extract for the base instead of Vanilla.

MINTY CHOCOLATE MOUNTAIN

BASE:

Extract (Mint) [*pg. 13*]

MIX-IN:

⅓ cup Chips (Chocolate Chips) [*pg. 34*]

20 Candy (Andes Mints) [*pg. 35*]

10 Cookie (Thin Mints or Grasshoppers) [*pg. 36*]

20 Brownie [*pg. 38*]

MODIFICATIONS:

Add as many or as few of the mix-ins as you want for this recipe. It's best when there's something crunchy (Cookie or Chips) with something chewy (Brownie). Either Girl Scout Thin Mint Cookies or Keebler Grasshoppers can work as the Cookie mix-in.

HERE'S THE SCOOP:

While it's difficult to not eat an entire box of Girl Scout Thin Mint Cookies, this recipe is worth it. If you're out of season for Girl Scout cookies, Keebler Grasshopers provide the same effect.

For an extra minty kick, you can also swap out the Andes mints for York Peppermint Patties. This minty combo of a mint base with York candies is my go-to when I order from Cold Stone Creamery.

Adding Chocolate Chips works for that satisfying crunch and a chewy Brownie mix-in is an excellent way to keep the minty flavor around a little longer.

If you're feeling adventurous, add all the mix-ins for a mountain of chocolate in a minty base. Just be sure to have a container big enough to hold it all!

Cherry Amaretto Chocolate Chip

Base:
Extract (Almond or Amaretto) [*pg. 13*]
Mix-in:
⅓ cup Chips (Chocolate Chips) [*pg. 34*]
1 ½ cup Fruit (Maraschino Cherry or Cherry) [*pg. 42*]
¼ cup Syrup Swirl (Maraschino Cherry) [*pg. 47*]
Modifications:
Use the syrup from a 10-ounce jar of maraschino cherries for the swirl. Also chop the cherries into quarters to add as a mix-in ¾ of the way through churning the base.

Here's the Scoop:
Unlike using regular cherries, maraschino cherries have enough sugar in them to prevent freezing. If you want to use fresh cherries instead, then follow the Fruit mix-in recipe for cherries. Using almond extract is a much stronger flavor than amaretto, but you decide which you prefer.

Candy Crunch

Base:
Candy (Lemon or Butterscotch) [*pg. 16*]
Mix-in:
20 Candy (Lemon or Butterscotch) [*pg. 35*]
Modifications:
None.

Here's the Scoop:
The crunchy mix-in contrasts the smooth base. Be sure to match the candy for the base and the mix-in.

CARAMEL CANDY APPLE

BASE:
Candy (Werther's Originals Caramel) [*pg. 16*]

MIX-IN:
1 ½ cup Fruit (Apple) [*pg. 42*]

MODIFICATIONS:
Use Granny Smith apples soaked in apple flavored brandy for the Fruit mix-in.

HERE'S THE SCOOP:
This recipe benefited from our discovery of alcohol-soaked fruit as well as perfecting the Candy base. You'll want to be sure to have a tart apple like a Granny Smith for this recipe, as anything too sweet won't contrast with the already sweet caramel base.

GINGERBREAD

BASE:
Candy (Cinnamon, Lemon, and Werther's Originals Caramel) [*pg. 16*]

MIX-IN:
10 Cookie (Gingersnaps) [*pg. 36*]

MODIFICATIONS:
Use 10 Cinnamon discs, 5 Lemon, and 5 Werther's Originals to get to 20 pieces for the Candy base. Add ½ teaspoon allspice to the sugar for the base.

Stop Screaming!

Here's the Scoop:
This recipe came about by accident when we had some random candies lying around and decided to make a base with it. The result tasted a lot like gingerbread because of the spicy cinnamon candies. After a few iterations of trying to recreate this recipe, we received some feedback to add allspice. It added some warmth to the taste that was missing in the original we had made.

Fruity Cheesecake

Base:
Cream Cheese [*pg. 18*]

Mix-in:
½ cup Graham Cracker [*pg. 38*]
1 ½ cup Fruit (Strawberry, Blueberry, or Cherry) [*pg. 42*]

Modifications:
None.

Here's the Scoop:
If you've had a fruit-based cheesecake before, just use that fruit as a mix-in and you'll be fine. We usually go with strawberry but you can do blueberries or cherries as well.

Horchata Rum

Base:
Granulated Flavor (Ground Cinnamon) [*pg. 19*]

Mix-in:
None.

MODIFICATIONS:
Replace 1 cup milk with 1 cup rice milk. Before churning, add 4 Tablespoons RumChata spirits.

HERE'S THE SCOOP:
I came across a cream liqueur known as RumChata while on a trip to Mexico to retrieve more of their delicious vanilla extract. This drink tastes like horchata and rum had a beautiful baby together. Considering that we already had a recipe for a cinnamon base, it wasn't difficult to make into a Horchata Rum ice cream.

As an ice cream, the Horchata Rum base pulls in the cinnamon and rice milk from its namesake and the Rum-Chata adds just a bit of an alcoholic kick. The result is something smooth that has been a perennial favorite at our Fourth of Jul-ice Cream social. The trick is that alcohol does not freeze and will require you to churn for longer than normal. Be sure to not add too much RumChata, otherwise you might end up with slush that won't set in the freezer.

SNICKERDOODLE

BASE:
Granulated Flavor (Ground Cinnamon) [*pg. 19*]
MIX-IN:
10 Cookie (Snickerdoodle) [*pg. 36*]
MODIFICATIONS:
Add ½ teaspoon cream of tartar to the Cinnamon base and use 1 less Tablespoon ground cinnamon.

Stop Screaming!

Here's the Scoop:
Adding the cream of tartar to the base replicates the flavor profile in the snickerdoodle cookies. And since there's already plenty of cinnamon in the Cookie mix-in, you can reduce the amount used in the base.

Tropical Sorbet

Base:
Juice Sorbet (Strawberry, Kiwi, & Dragon fruit) [*pg. 20*]

Mix-in:
None.

Modifications:
Using ⅔ pound strawberries, ⅔ pound kiwi, and ⅔ pound dragon fruit, boil all three fruits using the standard Juice Sorbet recipe.

Here's the Scoop:
Both Kiwi and Dragon fruit are unique flavors. Almost too unique. You'll usually find these tropical fruits paired with a more common fruit like strawberry. This recipe attempts to emulate that.

Blackberry White Chocolate Pudding

Base:
Juice Sorbet (Blackberry / Chocolate-covered Fruit) [*pg. 21*]

Mix-in:
None.

Modifications:

Use Hershey's White Chocolate pudding for the Chocolate-covered Fruit variation of this recipe.

Here's the Scoop:

My favorite recipe is Blackberry White Chocolate Pudding. This recipe came about partly by accident. First, we tried to make blackberry sorbet in the same way we made the raspberry sorbet. For some reason, it never quite set. The result was blackberry slush. We theorized that blackberries are a fruit common in northern latitudes where it's colder for longer portions of the year. Consequently, these berries have a natural antifreeze that causes them to not completely freeze. Your blackberries might not have this issue.

Next, we attempted to make a base out of white chocolate pudding. There's a dessert in my family known as "Chocolate Junk." It's just white chocolate pudding, a whole pan of brownies, an entire bag of crushed Heath bars, and a whole container of whipped cream mixed together. I figured the white chocolate pudding would be the base for this ice cream with the brownies and crushed Heath bars added as mix-ins (for the successful Chocolate Junk recipe, see Chocolate Dream Dessert [*pg. 71*]). When the white chocolate pudding froze hard as a rock, we knew it wasn't viable as a base. This is why you must wait until the hot fruit juice mixture is completely chilled before adding the pudding. Otherwise, the pudding will start solidifying as soon as it's mixed with the milk and cream.

Just like Goldilocks found one bed too soft and one bed too hard, we arrived at a solution for these two misbehaving bases. Mixing them together resulted in this recipe, which has the perfect consistency. In my opinion, this is the most unique and flavorful ice cream you will ever make. The blackberry hits your palate first, but then it develops into the taste of white chocolate pudding as it melts in your mouth. It's a complex flavor with a beautiful purple color and a perfect texture. When people ask what my favorite flavor is, this is my answer.

Honey Nut Blueberry Sherbet

BASE:
Juice Sorbet (Blueberry / Sherbet) [*pg. 21*]
MIX-IN:
¼ cup Nuts (Almonds) [*pg. 37*]
¼ cup Syrup Swirl (Honey) [*pg. 47*]
MODIFICATIONS:
Use the Sherbet variation of Juice Sorbet to lighten the strong Blueberry flavor.

HERE'S THE SCOOP:
With both Honey and Almonds as mix-ins in this book, it took us a while to figure out the right base to add this "Honey Nut" into. The strong flavor of Blueberry Sherbet seemed like a natural fit but needed the sherbet variation to lessen its boldness. Be sure to experiment with other Juice Sorbets if something else clicks better.

Mango Margarita Sorbet

BASE:
Pulp Sorbet (Mango / Margarita) [*pg. 24*]
MIX-IN:
None.

MODIFICATIONS:

Add 3 Tablespoons lime juice and use 3 Tablespoons tequila and 1 Tablespoon triple sec for the alcohol.

HERE'S THE SCOOP:

This recipe is strikingly simple, likely due to how close it is to just making a regular margarita and pouring it into an ice cream maker.

STRAWBERRY DAIQUIRÍ SHERBET

BASE:

Pulp Sorbet (Strawberry / Sherbet / Daiquirí) [*pg. 24*]

MIX-IN:

None.

MODIFICATIONS:

Add 3 Tablespoons lemon-lime soda and use 4 Tablespoons rum for the alcohol. Use the Sherbet variation of Pulp Sorbet.

HERE'S THE SCOOP:

While vacationing in Mexico, I made it a point to try every flavor of daiquirí available. I determined Strawberry was my favorite. Therefore, I chose this flavor for the daiquirí recipe. Making it into a Sherbet is a personal choice based on "berries and cream."

You can easily substitute Pineapple or Banana, but they both have a bit too much fiber in them and end up being a harder base than the Strawberry one is.

BANANA PUDDING

BASE:
Pulp Sorbet (Banana / Sherbet) [*pg. 24*]

MIX-IN:
10 Cookie (Nilla Wafers) [*pg. 36*]

MODIFICATIONS:
Use 4 Tablespoons rum to ensure the base does not freeze too hard.

HERE'S THE SCOOP:
Another one of those classic desserts, the Banana Pulp Sherbet might lean into daiquirí territory by itself. However, adding the Nilla Wafers into the mix recreates the banana pudding experience.

BIRTHDAY CAKE

BASE:
Cake Batter (Yellow Cake) [*pg. 27*]

MIX-IN:
⅓ cup Chips (Rainbow Sprinkles) [*pg. 34*]

MODIFICATIONS:
None.

HERE'S THE SCOOP:
This recipe benefits from the sprinkles dissolving in the base to add their little spots of color. The sprinkles also add that Funfetti effect that separates a standard yellow cake with a birthday cake.

CARROT CAKE

BASE:
Cake Batter (Spice Cake) [*pg. 27*]
MIX-IN:
¼ cup Nuts (Walnuts) [*pg. 37*]
¾ cup Fruit (Carrot) [*pg. 42*]
MODIFICATIONS:
Use half the amount of Fruit (¾ cup) and half the amount of vodka (⅛ cup) or other flavorless grain alcohols for the Carrot Fruit mix-in.

HERE'S THE SCOOP:
The Spice Cake does a lot of heavy lifting here, but it's important to note that the addition of the Carrots is more about the texture. Don't overdo it. In fact, halve the recipe.

PUMPKIN SPICE PIE

BASE:
Cake Batter (Spice Cake) [*pg. 27*]
MIX-IN:
¼ cup Graham Cracker [*pg. 38*]
MODIFICATIONS:
Add 1 cup of canned pumpkin puree and up to 2 Tablespoons whiskey to the Cake Batter base after adding the cake mix.

HERE'S THE SCOOP:
While pumpkin spice is all the rage in the fall, you don't have to get the right mixture of these spices for this recipe

STOP SCREAMING!

because the Cake Batter base takes care of it. Adding alcohol helps keep the mixture smooth with the added fibrous pumpkin in a base that also freezes harder than most.

RED VELVET

BASE:
Cake Batter (Red Velvet) [*pg. 27*]/Cream Cheese [*pg. 18*]
MIX-IN:
20 Brownie [*pg. 38*]
MODIFICATIONS:
If desired, follow the instructions for the Cake Batter base, substituting 8 ounces of softened cream cheese for a cup of heavy whipping cream. Blend the cream cheese and heavy cream until the mixture is smooth. Be sure to not blend too much, only enough to incorporate the cream cheese into the mixture.

HERE'S THE SCOOP:
Because Red Velvet was one of my favorite Ben & Jerry's flavors, we tried making this recipe early in our experiments. Unfortunately, we had an incident that made us reconsider this recipe for many years.

When we first tried a Red Velvet recipe, we dropped the bottle of red food coloring from the top of the refrigerator, and it exploded over our kitchen. I wish I had taken a picture because it legitimately looked like a murder scene. I focused on wiping down all the surfaces covered in this red coloring instead of documenting this moment. Using some hydrogen peroxide, we cleaned our kitchen and the nearby carpet sufficiently enough to prevent any red stains from remaining.

You'll notice that none of the recipes in this book contain much (if any) food coloring at all. This is the reason. Most of these recipes will come out white because of the amount of milk and cream involved. If you want to add some food coloring to incorporate some color into your recipes, go ahead, but be sure not to drop the bottle!

PANCAKES & SYRUP

BASE:
Cake Batter (Pancake Mix) [*pg. 27*]

MIX-IN:
¼ cup Syrup Swirl (Maple Syrup) [*pg. 47*]

MODIFICATIONS:
Use a Pancake or Waffle Mix that requires eggs for the Cake Batter base.

HERE'S THE SCOOP:
The butter in the Cake Batter base merely adds to the flavor profile for this breakfast treat. Be sure to use a Pancake or Waffle Mix that requires eggs, as many only need water and the recipe for the Cake Batter base already uses eggs.

As was mentioned in the Syrup Swirl section, this mix-in can be challenging to get reduced to the right amount. Don't fret if it freezes too hard or dissolves into the base, as it may take a try or two to hone in on the right viscosity of the syrup.

This recipe tastes a little chalky to me, but others seem to like it. Try substituting half the pancake mix for a plain cake batter mix if you also find this recipe to be a tad on the chalky side.

Lemon Meringue Pie

BASE:
Citrus Custard (Lemon) [*pg. 28*]
MIX-IN:
½ cup Meringue [*pg. 40*]
MODIFICATIONS:
None.

HERE'S THE SCOOP:
The Citrus Custard base really pops with the addition of the meringue mix-in, and you can leave this recipe with only that mix-in and it'll be great. However, if you want to recreate that pie crust texture, add some Graham Cracker mix-in as well.

Key Lime Pie

BASE:
Citrus Custard (Lime) [*pg. 28*]
MIX-IN:
½ cup Graham Cracker [*pg. 38*]
MODIFICATIONS:
None.

HERE'S THE SCOOP:
Much like the Lemon Meringue Pie above, you can easily attain the Key Lime Pie flavor by using limes as the Citrus Custard base. Be sure to include the Graham Cracker mix-in for that pie crust equivalent.

MOSCOW MULE

BASE:
Citrus Custard (Lime) [*pg. 28*]

MIX-IN:
¼ cup Syrup Swirl (Ginger Ale Soda) [*pg. 47*]

MODIFICATIONS:
Add a few Tablespoons (not more than 4) of whiskey to the base with the lime juice.

HERE'S THE SCOOP:
This alcoholic drink usually focuses on ginger beer with a lime accent. Flipping it around with the lime Citrus Custard and ginger ale Syrup Swirl still produces a somewhat similar result.

TRIPLE CHOCOLATE

BASE:
Chocolate [*pg. 30*]

MIX-IN:
⅓ cup Chips (Chocolate Chips) [*pg. 34*]
20 Brownie [*pg. 38*]

MODIFICATIONS:
None

HERE'S THE SCOOP:
It didn't take long for us to figure out how to make the highest density chocolate ice cream. I particularly like the chewiness of the brownies and the bit of crunch from the chocolate chips in this one.

Chocolate-Dipped Strawberries

BASE:
Chocolate [*pg. 30*]

MIX-IN:
⅓ cup Chips (Chocolate Chips) [*pg. 34*]
1 ½ cups Fruit (Strawberries) [*pg. 42*]

MODIFICATIONS:
None.

HERE'S THE SCOOP:
Chocolate-dipped fruit is a standard for fondue restaurant desserts. Even chocolate-dipped strawberries can be found at fancy dinners as well. If you want a bit of that chocolate shell crunch, add chocolate chips. Otherwise, this recipe can work with the Fruit as its only mix-in.

Toffee

BASE:
Chocolate [*pg. 30*]

MIX-IN:
20 Candy (Werther's Originals Caramels) [*pg. 35*]
¼ cup Nuts (Almonds) [*pg. 37*]

MODIFICATIONS:
Alternatively, if you want to leave out the nuts, use the Candy mix-in with Heath Bars, which are already toffee without almonds.

HERE'S THE SCOOP:
This simulated dessert relies on caramel candies and almonds to complete the toffee experience.

Chocolate Dream Dessert

BASE:
Chocolate (White Chocolate) [*pg. 30*]

MIX-IN:
20 Candy (Heath Bars) [*pg. 35*]
20 Brownie [*pg. 38*]

MODIFICATIONS:
None.

HERE'S THE SCOOP:
We refer to this family favorite recipe as "Chocolate Junk." It originally used white chocolate pudding (which is what eventually gave us the Blackberry White Chocolate Pudding recipe [*pg. 61*]). However, it's much easier to just use Baker's white chocolate for the base since pudding freezes too hard. Add a healthy dollop of whipped cream to each serving and enjoy!

Rocky Road

BASE:
Chocolate [*pg. 30*]

MIX-IN:
¼ cup Nuts (Almonds) [*pg. 37*]
½ cup Meringue (Marshmallow) [*pg. 40*]

MODIFICATIONS:
Sprinkle the almonds bits on the meringue before putting in the oven or leave as separate mix-ins.

HERE'S THE SCOOP:
While not a true Rocky Road, this recipe will get you

close. Marshmallow is notoriously difficult to work with, and several attempts at incorporating it as a mix-in were unsuccessful. Marshmallow-flavored meringue emulates the chewiness and taste of marshmallow, so this is as close as our homemade ice cream can get for now.

FAKE FISH FOOD

BASE:
  Chocolate [*pg. 30*]
MIX-IN:
  ⅓ cup Chips (Chocolate Chips) [*pg. 34*]
  ½ cup Meringue (Marshmallow) [*pg. 40*]
  ¼ cup Syrup Swirl (Caramel) [*pg. 47*]
MODIFICATIONS:
  Use larger Chocolate Chips than the suggested mini size.

HERE'S THE SCOOP:
  Another favorite Ben & Jerry's flavor from my childhood. This recipe combines all the elements of the original "Phish Food" flavor and gets somewhat close to the experience.

S'MORES

BASE:
  Chocolate [*pg. 30*]
MIX-IN:
  ½ cup S'mores [*pg. 45*]

MODIFICATIONS:

None.

HERE'S THE SCOOP:

This was one of the first "complicated" recipes we tried after learning how easy it was to make homemade ice cream. Because S'mores was one of my favorite Ben & Jerry's flavors, it shocked me at how close we could get this recipe to their version.

CHAPTER 5: SERVING/MENUS

With a couple dozen different ice cream recipes now under your belt, it's time to show off a little. This was the main reason we included a variety of ice creams for our housewarming party in 2015—we wanted people to try the flavors we had created. Our first Fourth of Jul-ice Cream had the following menu:

- Cherry Chocolate chip
- Double Chocolate
- Cinnamon
- Strawberry
- Vanilla

When our Fourth of Jul-ice Cream event became an annual tradition, we added a lot more flavors to the mix. Considering that there are 44 bases you can make in this book and 42 mix-ins, there are almost 1,900 combinations for solitary bases and single mix-in recipes. That number gets much larger with each mix-in you add. As of 2023, our menu for the event had more than tripled even if it was less than 1% of the available permutations:

- Thin Mint Cookies and Cream
- S'mores
- Toffee
- Fake Fish Food
- Chocolate Dream Dessert

- Red Velvet Brownie
- Cherry Amaretto Chocolate Chip
- Chocolate Chip Cookie Dough
- Crème Brûlée
- Key Lime Pie
- Gingerbread
- Horchata Rum
- Caramel Candy Apple
- Peaches and Cream Cheese
- Rhubarb Sorbet
- Tropical Sorbet
- Vanilla

For the first event, I didn't consider which order to serve them. Once we were serving flavors in the double digits, there needed to be a conscious transition from one flavor to another. This reduces shock to the palate and helps the overall experience of eating 17 different ice creams.

I often consider a menu of at least a dozen ice cream flavors to be like a wine tasting. There is a spectrum of flavor that covers a lot of ground. If you've ever done a wine tasting, the progression is usually dry to sweet. Since all ice creams are sweet, I progress from bitter to fruity. This means that I'll usually start at the chocolate bases and move my way into the sorbets via the fruit mix-ins. There's no "one size fits all" order for serving multiple ice creams, but this has worked for me.

Logistically, it helps to have a chest freezer to pull the individual containers and scoop from them when everyone has had a taste of the current flavor. It is also recommended to use small bowls and spoons—along with a melon baller as an ice cream scoop—to ensure the scoops you serve aren't too large. After all, if you're giving people over a dozen different scoops of ice cream, it can add up fast.

Below, you will find a few suggested serving menus you can use for your next tasting event. Just like a wine tasting, make sure that there is plenty of water and salty snacks (like pretzels) to cleanse the palate between each flavor.

Ice Cream Shop

MENU:

1. Chocolate [*pg. 30*]
2. Rocky Road [*pg. 71*]
3. Minty Chocolate Mountain (Chocolate Chip) [*pg. 55*]
4. Christmas in July [*pg. 54*]
5. Cherry Amaretto Chocolate Chip [*pg. 56*]
6. Cake Batter (Yellow Cake) [*pg. 26*]
7. Candy (Butterscotch) [*pg. 16*]
8. Fruit & Cream (Strawberry) [*pg. 53*]
9. Fruity Cheesecake (Strawberry) [*pg. 58*]
10. Candy (Cotton Candy Saltwater Taffy) [*pg. 16*]
11. Juice Sorbet (Raspberry) [*pg. 20*]
12. Extract (Vanilla) [*pg. 13*]

HERE'S THE SCOOP:

We all have memories of going to get ice cream. While places like Baskin Robbins have 31 flavors, a solid dozen are common across all ice cream shops. This list isn't necessarily in perfect order as you aren't supposed to eat all the flavors at an ice cream shop in succession. Still, there are enough similarities between adjacent flavors to not create any palate whiplash.

DESSERT DUPLICATES

MENU:
1. Triple Chocolate [*pg. 69*]
2. S'mores [*pg. 72*]
3. Toffee [*pg. 70*]
4. Cookies & Cream (Oreo) [*pg. 51*]
5. Crème Brûlée [*pg. 53*]
6. Cake Batter (Yellow Cake) [*pg. 27*]
7. Red Velvet [*pg. 66*]
8. Fruity Cheesecake (Strawberry) [*pg. 58*]
9. Caramel Candy Apple [*pg. 57*]
10. Pumpkin Spice Pie [*pg. 65*]
11. Lemon Meringue Pie [*pg. 68*]
12. Candy (Cotton Candy Saltwater Taffy) [*pg. 16*]

HERE'S THE SCOOP:
Many of the inspirations for the recipes in this book were born from classic desserts. Brownies appear in Triple Chocolate. S'mores is a standard for any camping trip. Toffee is great for a crunchy dessert. Who hasn't sat down after dinner and eaten a whole sleeve of Oreos? Or, if you're fancier, you've ordered the Crème Brûlée at an expensive restaurant. Even a classic slice of Yellow Cake is a recipe for nostalgia. Of course, we shouldn't ignore the modern Red Velvet craze either if we're talking about cake. Then there's a Fruity Cheesecake if you want to introduce a little fruity flavor to the mix. A Caramel Candy Apple is as much a fall treat as a flavorful Pumpkin Spice Pie. And if you're in the mood for pie, then nothing beats a Lemon Meringue

Stop Screaming!

Pie. Finally, you can taste light and flavorful Cotton Candy through the Candy recipe.

Chocoholics Anonymous

MENU:
1. Triple Chocolate [*pg. 69*]
2. Red Velvet [*pg. 66*]
3. S'mores [*pg. 72*]
4. Toffee [*pg. 70*]
5. Minty Chocolate Mountain (Brownie and Chocolate Chips) [*pg. 55*]
6. Cookies & Cream (Oreo) [*pg. 51*]
7. Rocky Road [*pg. 71*]
8. Fake Fish Food [*pg. 72*]
9. Cherry Amaretto Chocolate Chip [*pg. 56*]
10. Chocolate-Dipped Strawberries [*pg. 70*]
11. Blackberry White Chocolate Pudding [*pg. 60*]
12. Chocolate Dream Dessert [*pg. 71*]

HERE'S THE SCOOP:

For those who cannot get enough chocolate, here is a list of a dozen recipes to serve in succession. You start out with the most chocolate-intensive recipe, Triple Chocolate. Shift into a rich chocolate base by using a Red Velvet cake mix with the Cake Batter base. By the time you get to S'mores, you'll add in some marshmallow that transitions the nuts in the Toffee, which is next in the list. Since Minty Chocolate Mountain does not use chocolate as its base, it's a simple transition to Cookies and Cream. This still favors chocolate flavor, albeit through its Oreo mix-in. Re-introducing the nutty flavor, we have the classic Rocky Road next. The crunchy nuts and chewy marshmallow in Rocky

Road easily shift into the caramel swirled chocolate chip Fake Fish Food. Cherry Amaretto Chocolate Chip introduces fruit flavors into the mix. Then switch to Chocolate-Dipped Strawberries and a white chocolate infused Blackberry Sorbet. Continuing the white chocolate theme, the last ice cream is none other than Chocolate Dream Dessert. This has the same brownie and chocolate chip texture that can lead you back to the Triple Chocolate at the beginning of the list, if so desired.

Fruitylicious

MENU:
1. Blackberry White Chocolate Pudding [*pg. 60*]
2. Fruity Cheesecake (Strawberry) [*pg. 58*]
3. Cherry Amaretto Chocolate Chip [*pg. 56*]
4. Fruit & Cream (Peach) [*pg. 53*]
5. Caramel Candy Apple [*pg. 57*]
6. Harvest Pie [*pg. 52*]
7. Key Lime Pie [*pg. 68*]
8. Candy Crunch (Lemon) [*pg. 56*]
9. Juice Sorbet (Raspberry) [*pg. 20*]
10. Pulp Sorbet (Rhubarb) [*pg. 23*]
11. Mango Margarita Sorbet [*pg. 62*]
12. Tropical Sorbet [*pg. 60*]

HERE'S THE SCOOP:
There are a lot of options for fruit-flavored ice cream. If you want to try them all (with minimal repeating fruits), this is the menu for you. While some of these recipes are fruit in their pure form (i.e., the sorbets), there is enough variety in the bases to make things interesting. From the

STOP SCREAMING!

ever-unique Blackberry Sorbet with White Chocolate Pudding to Caramel Candy Apple, most of these recipes feature a single fruit flavor—even if it's occasionally artificial (like in Lemon Candy Crunch). Harvest Pie and Tropical Sorbet are the only items on this menu that have multiple fruits. Fruit is not necessarily the easiest mix-in to deal with, so if you successfully serve this full menu, give yourself a pat on the back!

Super Sorbets and Sherbets

MENU:
1. Juice Sorbet (Raspberry) [*pg. 20*]
2. Tropical Sorbet [*pg. 60*]
3. Juice Sorbet (Cranberry) [*pg. 20*]
4. Honey Nut Blueberry Sherbet [*pg. 62*]
5. Juice Sorbet (Cherry / Chocolate-covered) [*pg. 21*]
6. Blackberry White Chocolate Pudding [*pg. 60*]
7. Pulp Sorbet (Peach) [*pg. 23*]
8. Mango Margarita Sorbet [*pg. 62*]
9. Pulp Sorbet (Pineapple / Daiquirí) [*pg. 24*]
10. Pulp Sorbet (Rhubarb) [*pg. 23*]
11. Pulp Sorbet (Honeydew) [*pg. 23*]
12. Pulp Sorbet (Watermelon) [*pg. 23*]

HERE'S THE SCOOP:

For a cookbook about ice cream, there are a lot of options for sorbets and sherbets. After all, if it's a fruit, you can likely make a sorbet out of it. While there's not much dairy in these recipes, at least half of this list has alcohol in it. You can get away without either gluten, dairy, or alcohol in most of these recipes if you have guests with dietary restrictions. Just be sure to make a test batch ahead of time to ensure the result doesn't freeze too hard for when you eventually serve it.

Taste The Rainbow

MENU:
1. Pulp Sorbet (Rhubarb) [*pg. 23*]
2. Red Velvet [*pg. 66*]
3. Mango Margarita Sorbet [*pg. 62*]
4. Cake Batter (Yellow Cake) [*pg. 27*]
5. Candy (Cotton Candy Saltwater Taffy) [*pg. 16*]
6. Juice Sorbet (Blueberry) [*pg. 20*]
7. Blackberry White Chocolate Pudding [*pg. 60*]

HERE'S THE SCOOP:
Even though we have an aversion to food coloring in our house, this menu uses natural (and some artificial) coloring to create a rainbow of ice cream. Be sure to use pink stalks for the Rhubarb Sorbet to create the pink color needed for the first item on this menu. Red Velvet might use artificial coloring, but it's a rich red color that's hard to duplicate. With its striking orange color, Mango Sorbet is one of the most stunning natural colors you'll come across in this menu. Cake Batter is a little lighter shade of yellow when you use a Yellow Cake mix, but it still comes across. Cotton Candy Saltwater Taffy also has a faint green to greenish blue color that comes from the artificial coloring of the saltwater taffy. Blueberry Sorbet is a deep blue color that borders on black. Blackberry White Chocolate Pudding has a rich purple color that can only be made through the natural blackberry dye mixing with the white chocolate pudding. Lining up all seven of these ice creams makes for a great photo opportunity to show off your skills!

INDEX

Stop Screaming!

ACKNOWLEDGEMENTS

First, I want to acknowledge that none of this would have been possible had we not received the ice cream maker attachment for our wedding from my Uncle Jim Dwight. I did not know that this would become such an involved hobby for me and my wife when we asked for the attachment. And yet, here we are.

Of course, I wouldn't be able to write all this down if it weren't for the tireless efforts of my wife, Laura. Her dedication to this hobby over the years has always astonished me with its results. I love collaborating on new recipes and techniques as we advance our ice cream knowledge. That I finally asked her enough times to write these recipes down so I could share them with the world is the reason you now hold this book in your hand.

Each year, we hold our annual Fourth of Jul-ice Cream event at our house. I must acknowledge the kind words and curious guests who came for free samples of these recipes. They are what inspired me to write this book.

Most of our friends and family do not know how easy homemade ice cream is to make, and I love telling them the secrets of our successful recipes. Specifically, I want to give a tremendous shout out to Barb Kramer, Julie Weilert, Andy Weilert, and Dan Weilert, who have tested these recipes. They made sure my instructions were clear and would work in kitchens that were not my own.

Finally, Michael Olson created the outstanding cover art for this book. You can follow him on Instagram at @michaelolsonart.

ABOUT THE AUTHOR

14er Climber
Rocket Scientist
Published Novelist
Movie Connoisseur
Stock Photographer

Benjamin M. Weilert is an award-winning multi-genre writer from Colorado who writes whatever stories pop into his head. He is on a mission to write something in every single genre...eventually.

Currently, he has written a Young Adult science fantasy trilogy (*The Fluxion Trilogy*), a memoir about climbing Colorado's 14,000-foot peaks with his father (*Fourteener Father*), a guidebook to movies (*Cinema Connections*), a children's picture book (*This is Not a Drill*), a hard science fiction survival story (*Buried Colony*), and many other short stories that have been published in anthologies—as well as his *The Ascent of the Writer* collection.

Every novel he has ever written has been during National Novel Writing Month (NaNoWriMo). He has won the challenge 12 times in a row and plans to win for many more years to come. Currently, he is the Municipal Liaison for the Colorado Springs region: helping other novelists find their stories and write them down.

He currently lives in Colorado Springs with his supporting wife and children. You can find him online on social media as "BMW the Author."

For more information, please visit:
author.benjamin-m-weilert.com

FOURTEENER FATHER

A memoir of life above 14,000 ft.

Hardcover | Paperback | eBook

When does a hobby become an obsession?

Colorado has 58 mountains that tower above the landscape. 58 mountains that, when combined together, hold a certain amount of prestige amongst the natives. 58 mountains that have summits above 14,000 feet. These mountains are collectively known as the "fourteeners." As beautiful

as Colorado is, its mountains have a certain addicting quality that keeps us coming back for more.

This is a story of a father and son who managed to climb them all...together. Along the way, they dodged lightning, escaped mudslides, and slid down snowfields (both accidentally and on purpose). Over 32 years, this father-son duo grew as hikers and as men. Their experiences helped them bond and resulted in an emotional climax that will leave you in tears.

For anyone who is a son or a father, this book gives an insight into the lives of a father and son who did all right. Filled with inspiration, adventure, and love, *Fourteener Father* is a journey through all that Colorado's fourteeners have to offer.

CINEMA CONNECTIONS
A never-ending "6 Degrees of Kevin Bacon"
Hardcover | Paperback | eBook

No movie is an island.
How often do you open up Netflix and wonder, "What do I want to watch?" Have you ever seen a movie that was so great, you want more of it? Well, look no further than this book. *Cinema Connections* is a guide through at least 400 movies connected to each other in some very unique ways. These aren't the *1001 Movies*

You Must See Before You Die, but they might just point you in the direction of your next favorite film.

Written over seven years as a weekly blog, *Cinema Connections* is more than the sum of its parts. While this book contains the 400 posts that composed the online blog, it references 1,859 unique movies and has 3,692 connections between them. While not every movie in this book is critically-acclaimed, they are all connected to each other in some way...

...and to Kevin Bacon.

THIS IS NOT A DRILL
A picture book about tools and tool safety
Hardcover | Paperback | eBook

Robbie Robin's home blew down in a storm. You can build him a new birdhouse by following the instructions in *This is Not a Drill*.

Benjamin M. Weilert

Follow along as each tool used to build a birdhouse is discussed in this picture book for kids. *This is Not a Drill* asks children to identify the tools needed to construct a simple birdhouse while also providing parents with step-by-step instructions that they can use to build this birdhouse with their kids. As is the case with any tools, safety is identified throughout the book so children can learn how to use tools without getting hurt.

A great book for kids aged 2-6—and kids at heart—*This is Not a Drill* asks the important questions in life, like, "Is this a Drill?"

If you prefer fiction, here are the fictional works Benjamin M. Weilert has published...

FLUXION TRILOGY
Young Adult (YA) Science Fantasy
Omnibus Edition
Hardcover | Paperback | eBook

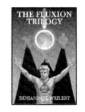

FIRST NAME BASIS
Book 1 of *The Fluxion Trilogy*
Paperback | eBook | Audiobook

SECOND TO NONE
Book 2 of *The Fluxion Trilogy*
Paperback | eBook | Audiobook

THE THIRD DEGREE
Book 3 of *The Fluxion Trilogy*
Paperback | eBook | Audiobook

BURIED COLONY
Interplanetary Survival Hard Sci-fi
Paperback | eBook

THE ASCENT OF
THE WRITER

Poems, articles, and short stories
Paperback | eBook

Sign up for the monthly newsletter on his website (under the "Connect" section), to receive a free eBook version!

DOMESTICATED
VELOCIRAPTORS

"Jurassic Manor" short story

LAST SHOT
FIRED

"Soul Photographer" short story

WELCOME TO
THE ALPACALYPSE

"Be Fruitful…" short story

CROSSING
BORDERS

"From c² Shining c" short story

THE FORGOTTEN
SHIFTER FILES

"Kami's Curse" short story

Printed in Great Britain
by Amazon